In a day in which we are overrun with 'cultural Christianity,' it's no wonder that many are confused about what it means to be an authentic follower of Jesus Christ . . . In *Things I've Learned on the Way to Heaven*, my friend Bill Thrasher brings clarity to the confusion. You will be refreshed by the God-focus of this book and the clear, compelling message of our great salvation!

> Dr. Crawford W. Loritts, Jr.
> Author, Speaker, Radio Host
> Associate Director, Campus Crusade for Christ, USA

I wish I could motivate every church attender to read and take to heart the message in this book. Motivated by his own journey to genuine faith after years of being deluded about what it means to be a Christian, Bill Thrasher challenges professing Christians to examine the reality of their spiritual condition in light of the Word of God.

> Nancy Leigh DeMoss
> Life Action Ministries

How refreshing to find the rich, historic teachings of the faith revealed in such a simple, personal and understandable way. If only every seeker and believer alike could read this book early in their spiritual pilgrimage.

> Randy Pope
> Senior Pastor
> Perimeter Church, Duluth, GA

THINGS I'VE LEARNED *on the* WAY TO HEAVEN

WILLIAM L. THRASHER JR.

MOODY PRESS

CHICAGO

All Scripture quotations, unless otherwise indicated, are taken from the *Holy Bible, New Living Translation*, copyright © 1996. Used by permission of Tyndale House Publishers, Inc., Wheaton Illinois 60189, U.S.A. All rights reserved.

Scripture quotations marked NIV are taken from the *Holy Bible, New International Version®*. NIV®. Copyright © 1973, 1978, 1984 by International Bible Society. Used by permission of Zondervan Publishing House. All rights reserved.

Scripture quotations marked NKJV are taken from the *New King James Version*. Copyright © 1982 by Thomas Nelson, Inc. Used by permission. All rights reserved.

Library of Congress Cataloging-in-Publication Data

Thrasher, William L.
    Things I've learned on the way to heaven / William L. Thrasher Jr.
        p. cm.
    ISBN 0-8024-3745-1
    1. Christian life—Biblical teaching. 2. Bible—Theology. I. Title.

BS680.C47 T48 2001
248.4—dc21

2001038167

1 3 5 7 9 10 8 6 4 2

Printed in the United States of America

With eternal thankfulness, this book is dedicated
to my heavenly Father,
to my Lord and Savior Jesus Christ,
and to the precious Holy Spirit.
Soli Deo gloria
(glory to God alone)

When I've been there ten thousand years,
I'll have no fewer days to sing God's praises
than when I first began.
Amazing grace! Amazing grace!
Sola gratia
(grace alone)

IN MEMORY

In the course of my writing this book, one of the giants of
the evangelical church, Dr. James Montgomery Boice,
went home to be with his Lord. He was used by God as one
of the most influential people in my growth in the faith.
I will be forever thankful to God for the privilege to learn
from one whose consuming passion was to glorify God
and to model the life of a disciple of Jesus Christ.

CONTENTS

FOREWORD

*T*his simple but provocative little book sets forth some vital evangelical truths that are too often ignored or forgotten these days. This is a succinct and timely treatment of some core doctrines that the 21st-century church cannot afford to let go of.

Bill Thrasher has a unique ability to summarize and explain sometimes difficult ideas in language and imagery that is profound and yet easy to grasp. In particular, this book features some important but too often neglected aspects of the gospel, handling these great truths with a rich simplicty that will be appreciated by young Christians and seasoned theologians alike.

The gospel is a call to conversion and newness of life. And yet it also teaches that sinners are helpless to convert themselves or change their lives. It therefore instructs the sinner to cast himself on the mercy of a sovereign God and trust God alone for a new heart, for forgiveness and justification, and for the power to live a transformed life.

This book highlights those God-centered, Christ-exalting aspects of the gospel, and for that I am deeply grateful. It brings God's work in salvation back into the spotlight where it belongs. It challenges the man-centered tendencies that are so popular in modern religion. As you read, may it also provoke you to higher thoughts about God and a deeper understanding of the gospel.

JOHN MACARTHUR

PREFACE

*I*n a sense, I have been writing this book for the past twenty-plus years. It began with my personal encounter with the triune God of the Bible and how that event permanently altered my life. This book represents one of the life messages God put on my heart. It is a true testimony of what happened in the life of one "unconverted believer" (more on that later) when God poured on him the amazing grace that brings about true salvation.

From the very beginning of my walk with Christ, I knew things were different. My thoughts, my focus, my preoccupation had been changed dramatically. Within days of my conversion—my personal "Damascus Road" experience—I began to read and study the Bible with a determined focus. I wanted to better understand what had taken place in my life, as well as the God who brought those things about. My hunger to learn the truth became an obsession, and, thankfully, that has never changed.

I remember reading the book of Romans over and over. As

I read, I began to understand what had happened at my transformation. I also began to see why I had been so blinded before my conversion. I realized that I had been spiritually dead to God, even though I had, over the years, demonstrated an interest in spiritual things. I learned that Satan, who desired that I never see the light of truth, did all he could to blind me to that truth.

God chose to meet me in a most unusual setting: thousands of miles from my native country, completely out of the religious environment I had grown to be a part of, and isolated from any close family or friends. During and shortly after the time of my conversion, it was just me and my wife, our Bibles, and the Holy Spirit of God. It was in this setting that God determined I would begin my journey as a true believer, and in this setting that He would help me to more fully comprehend what it means to be "born again." Immediately, my life was turned around to the point that it was obvious to all that something monumental, something beyond myself, had just taken place.

In retrospect, I believe that He met me when and where He did so that I would be forced to go to the Bible—the only source of truth concerning what God says about the condition of those who are lost in their sins and about what He has done to rescue them.

It was also by God's providence that no person, church, denomination, or group influenced my wife and me at that time. That forced us to continually cry out to God the Holy Spirit to help us, guide us, and give us understanding and direction. I am convinced this helped us establish a long-term pattern of striving to test and examine everything we receive and hear using the Word of God as our standard.

Our first outside exposure to spiritual guidance and teaching came when we were exposed, through audiotapes, to the preaching of John MacArthur. God used his love and passion for and faithful exposition of the Word to lay the foundation for our journey of faith.

All of this learning and growing brought us to a point where we had to tell others what we had learned.

TIME TO SHARE

God has brought me to a place where I want to share what I have learned. I have written this book for two broad audiences. The first group is truly born-again believers who desire to better understand the wondrous process of salvation. I also want to equip these believers with a clear and well-developed presentation so that they can become more effective witnesses to those around them who may not be truly converted believers.

I have also written this book for the millions of people who wrongly believe they know God and thus consider themselves Christians. These are people who are confident they are on their way to heaven. Many of them attend church regularly, and most, if not all, own Bibles and have some knowledge of what is in those Bibles. Most of these people say they pray on occasion, and some have a "special" feeling that God has been very close to them. Many of these people have a confidence in their faith based on how they are living, compared with others who are obviously lost and living a life of overt sin.

Another element of their confidence rests in the fact that at some point in their life they made a decision, walked down a church aisle, responded to an invitation at a crusade, joined a church, or even were baptized. They look to something they did as a child or in their youth as proof that they are truly born again.

From outward appearances, these people appear to be true believers. Tragically, however, they are living their lives deceived. They are not on their way to heaven, but instead on the broad road that leads to destruction. They are, in fact, blinded to the truth of their condition. They have false hope and are living a false life, and if they do not experience a miraculous transformation, they will die in their sins. They will spend eternity in hell, not heaven.

I believe I am well qualified to write this book, because for twenty-eight years I was one of those people I just described. Since my true conversion more than two decades ago, I have spent a great deal of time thinking about my season of deception. Now I want to share what I have learned about God, about the problem of sin and its horrible consequences, and about the wonderful plan of salvation that God provided for lost sinners like me.

By God's providence and for His purposes, He has provided me with an understanding of the clear contrast between the unconverted believer, which I used to be, and a true believer, which I am now.

If you want to go to heaven to be with God someday, I hope you will read on. By God's grace, I've learned a lot of things on the way to heaven, and I would like to share them with you.

ACKNOWLEDGMENTS

First and foremost, I want to thank the triune God of the Bible for giving me the opportunity, the circumstances of life, and the strength and abilities that have helped me in writing this book.

In some ways, writing a book can be compared to building a piece of furniture. To begin, both require raw material that God created and by His grace made available for their respective use. The furniture builder requires the wood that comes from trees, the tools that shape the wood, and the craftsmanship to create the end result of a thing of beauty.

A writer uses the gift of words and thoughts, capturing those thoughts in sentences and paragraphs. Most important is the truth that God has made available in the Bible, which should always be the ultimate foundation for everything that is written.

As the book begins to take shape, it will be strongly influenced by the thoughts and input from many others. Hopefully, at the completion of the writing there will be a solid and complete manuscript. But like a rough piece of furniture, there is still a lot of work required before the final product is ready to be called complete. It is only by the labor of many others that a book comes to completion, and it is through their contribution that the sparkle and polish are added that bring out the richness of the core material.

With that process in mind, I would like to recognize those who have given input and suggestions and others who have added the finishing sparkle and polish to this book.

I begin with great appreciation to Greg Thornton, my publisher, for his valuable suggestions, encouragement, and shared vision that he has given me on this project. I would also like to thank Michael Briggs, whom God has used to provide wise counsel on direction of this writing project.

I want to thank Tracy Sumner and Cheryl Dunlop for their excellent editorial work and for the opportunity to work with skilled craftsmen such as they.

Encouragement and feedback are always so important in the writing process, and special thanks go to Janis Backing and John Hinkley for their valuable input, as well as George Peterson and Dave DeWit for their excitement on reading the manuscript.

I also thank Dr. John Armstrong, who has been such an influence on my life in the area of reformation and revival. His passion and love for the truth continue to motivate and encourage me.

Last, but by no means least, thanks to my wonderful wife and life partner who, as always, played such a critical role in my writing. I want to especially recognize her for the work she did to select key Scripture references and then to note them throughout the manuscript. Most of all I thank her for her prayers and for her words of encouragement, and the sparkle and polish she adds to me.

INTRODUCTION

$\mathscr{I}$t is my hope that just the title of this book will stimulate questions from readers who may be examining their beliefs on the subject of eternity and where they think they will spend eternity. If the question of your eternal destination is of interest to you, if you want to be certain that heaven will be your eternal dwelling, then I hope you will find this book helpful.

There are millions of people who falsely think they are on their way to heaven. Many can even explain why they believe that when, in fact, they are headed the wrong way without even realizing it.

I can identify well with those millions because at one time I was one of them. I could say with great conviction that heaven would be my eternal destination, only to learn that I was on the "broad road that leads to destruction" (Matthew 7:13).

Some people have a hope of heaven's existence and think they may be lucky enough to make it there. They believe they will end up in heaven because on what they see as God's grading scale, their good deeds must surely outweigh their bad deeds. Others give little thought to the matter of eternal destination at all, trusting that because God is love and overlooks sin, eventually everyone gets there anyway. Still others believe Satan's lie that we only exist in this life—that when we die, it is over because there is no such thing as heaven or hell. Even within Christian circles some doubt eternal punishment.

It is sobering to realize that eternity lasts forever. In light of that, from a human perspective, the most important question we must ask ourselves is, "Where will I spend my eternity?" There are only two possible answers to that question. The Bible makes it clear that everyone who has been or ever will be born will either spend eternity with God in heaven or with the devil in hell.

Satan's primary goal is to destroy anything that gives God glory. Therefore, he will do whatever he can to blind and deceive those creatures made in the image of God and keep them from the truth of God's Word, which provides direction to heaven.

I have learned many great truths from the Bible, and among them is what God requires of a person who wants to go to heaven. God has provided clear instructions for anyone who is interested in spending eternity with Him, but He has also given substantial warnings about the things that will hinder someone from reaching heaven. God has laid out numerous and definitive roadmarks that can guide us on our journey to heaven, and He has also told us how we can have assurance that we will spend eternity with Him.

Endless numbers of people would have us believe they have some unique insight or new perspective on the truth about God. Actually, this has been the case throughout all of history, but with the introduction of the "Information Age," large segments of the population can access a staggering amount of information on nearly any subject. For example, you need only look at your local secular bookstore to see all sorts of materials on the subject of God. Tragically, however, much, if not most, of this material is the fabrication of someone's imagination and is devoid of real truth.

Much of the writing on God today ignores one monumental fact: The Bible is the *only* written source God Himself has given us to help us know about Him. Throughout the ages, many have claimed to have new or additional information pertaining to God. But the Scriptures warn us against adding to or taking away from the declared truth of the written Word of God.

The Bible is also the only source of truth concerning how we as lost sinners—dead to the things of God—can be born again to eternal life and enjoy renewed fellowship with the Almighty.

My purpose in writing this book is to explain, restate, and reinforce the ageless truth that God has chosen to reveal Himself in the pages of Scripture. It is in the Bible that He unfolds the story of His plan to redeem for Himself a people who will worship and adore Him and enjoy Him for all eternity.

There can be no doubting God's statement that unless a person is born again from above and becomes converted by faith and repentance, he or she will neither see nor enter His kingdom. There is one mediator between God and mankind, and He is Christ Jesus (1 Timothy 2:5). He is the only way, He is the only ultimate truth, and He is the only source of life. No one comes to God the Father but through Him (John 14:6).

I purposely wrote this book with a God-centered focus. This is of great importance to me because, in our day, we have become strongly creature-focused—even when it pertains to the things of God. We have become consumed with "self" in that we tend to approach God with an eye toward what He can do for us. In contrast, the Bible tells us we must approach God correctly if He is ever to respond to our overtures.

The Bible starts with God and ends with God. The Bible has more than fifteen thousand references to God. It tells us everything we need to know about God, including how He will accomplish His great plan of redemption.

Everyone needs to know that the main purpose of creation is to reveal almighty God and the work He has accomplished through the Lord Jesus Christ and through the Holy Spirit's work of regeneration.

That is the purpose of this book.

One

AN AWARENESS
OF GOD

*Oh, the depth of the riches both of the wisdom and
knowledge of God! How unsearchable are His judgments
and His ways past finding out! "For who has known the
mind of the Lord? Or who has become His counselor? Or
who has first given to Him and it shall be repaid to him?"
For of Him and through Him and to Him are all things,
to whom be glory forever. Amen.*

ROMANS 11:33–36 NKJV

Knowing God involves, first, listening to God's word and receiving it as the Holy Spirit interprets it, in application to oneself; second, noting God's nature and character, as His word and works reveal it; third, accepting His invitations, and doing what He commands; fourth, recognizing, and rejoicing in, the love that He has shown in thus approaching one and drawing one into this divine fellowship.

— J. I. PACKER

AN AWARENESS
OF GOD

*O*ne of the most profound truths I have learned over the past twenty-one years is the fact that the Lord God Almighty, the God of the Bible, is a sovereign God. When I learned this truth, I was truly blessed with an awareness of the true and living God.

The word *sovereignty* simply means that God is God. It means He is Most High and exalted above everything and that He is all-powerful, omnipotent, and able to do anything that is consistent with His character. God has absolute authority and rules over everything. He has supreme power over the entire universe and everything in it, and He is all-knowing and absolutely free from any external force.

The doctrine of the sovereignty of God is central to a correct understanding of all other doctrines. It is also a wonderful comfort for true believers to know that God is on His throne in heaven working "all things according to the counsel of His own will" (Ephesians 1:11 NKJV).

I know and am grateful for the fact that God is working out His plan and His purposes—which He set forth before the foundation of the world—in my life and in all of human history. It is through those plans and purposes that He will bring glory to Himself by the display of His wondrous love, grace, and mercy in salvation. He will do that while at the same time maintaining His absolute demand for justice against all sin, because He is holy and perfect in His righteousness.

I have learned from my study of the God of the Bible that He displays His sovereignty in three key areas that impact everyone, the first of which is in His creation.

SOVEREIGN IN HIS CREATION

Nothing exists that God did not create. By His word, He created the universe and everything in it. He created the billions of galaxies in the universe and the billions of stars each galaxy contains. He created the atom, the building block of matter. He masterminded the amazing balance of the earth in its relationship to the sun, allowing for the formation and continuance of life.

God has ordered it so that His laws of science govern the physical universe, yet He has demonstrated that He Himself exists above and beyond those laws. He was complete in Himself before creation and dependent on nothing and no one. He has no needs.

By right of creation, God the Creator is the sole owner of all things and has the prerogative to exercise His sovereign purpose and plan over all that He has made. God is Lord over the weather, the sun, the moon, and the stars. He is Lord over the devil and his demons. And finally, He is Lord over those made in His image—mankind. Nothing is outside of God's control.

This brings us to the second area in which God displays His sovereignty, and that is in His control over circumstances—His providence, or, to put it another way, the fact that He controls all things.

SOVEREIGN IN HIS PROVIDENCE

It is by God's providence that all things happen the way they do. He is the controlling power that sustains and shapes human destiny, yet He accomplishes this in a way that allows us the freedom He has given us.

Nothing can take God by surprise. Satan's rebellion did not surprise Him, nor did the fall of Adam and Eve in the Garden of Eden. God not only allowed these things, but in His providence He has used them for the ultimate benefit of His eternal kingdom.

One of the great biblical examples of God's providence is the story of Joseph. This account shows us very clearly that God had a plan, and that part of that plan was permitting evil to transpire on the part of men who acted out of sinful selfishness. God was in control in this situation and used what was an act of evil on the part of Joseph's brothers as His means to do good in the life of Joseph (Genesis 50:20).

The ultimate fulfillment of God's plan—in the context of history and within our individual lives—is possible because from the beginning of time He is in complete control and has perfect knowledge of all things. I have seen examples of this in my own life.

I can see now how God ordered events in my life in ways that ultimately worked toward an appointed time for Him to change my heart and my direction. Not all of those events came as a result of "good" done by me or to me. Many of the circumstances God used—and still uses, even as I write this book—to shape my life and bring about His purposes and plans came as a result of my own sinfulness or that of others. That is how God's providence works.

I now understand that God predetermined when and where I would be born, who would be my parents, and what kinds of influences would help shape my life. I know that for a time He allowed me to remain blinded to the real truth of my lost condition and to lose time I could have used to serve Him. But I also know that He did these things for a purpose: His ultimate glory.

At no time was I ever forced to do anything that was against God's revealed will. I practiced sinful deeds because it was consistent with my fallen nature. And this brings me to the third key area where God exercises and displays His sovereignty, and that is in His act of reaching down and giving wicked humans eternal life.

SOVEREIGN IN SALVATION

The Bible plainly states that before the foundation of the world God chose those whose names would be written in the Lamb's Book of Life (Revelation 17:8). In one sense, that is when all of those who would ever be reborn into God's kingdom were saved. This is where we see the sovereignty of God with regard to salvation. We know nothing more about *how* God chooses, but we must embrace this part of His sovereignty because it is part of God's revealed truth.

This truth demonstrates that salvation is *all* of God. It shows that it is only by God's choice that some of His creatures will receive the new spiritual heart that enables them to respond to the gospel and come to salvation by repenting and putting their faith in the Lord Jesus Christ. Without God's direct intervention in the lives of lost sinners, they would never depart from the broad road that leads to hell. Of course, God's sovereignty is His side of the picture and has no bearing on our responsibility before Him—He calls all to repent and believe.

Twenty-one years ago, God showed me that I was lost and on that broad road. I saw what I had never seen before: my own sinfulness and how lost I had been. This frightening realization overwhelmed me. I was stunned at what was going on in my mind. At that time, I received His gift of salvation. From the moment of my conversion, I knew everything in me had changed. I felt inexpressible joy as I sensed that God had poured His love all over me.

I have never gotten over that moment. I am still so thankful to the merciful God who in His sovereignty chose to meet me and make me a new creation, and who chose to bring me into His family and allow me to play a role in building His kingdom.

This, to me, is a demonstration of God's sovereignty in my own life. God saved me and caused me to grow, because He wanted to use me to communicate to others what true salvation really is.

COMMUNICATING TRUE SALVATION

Since the day God welcomed me into His kingdom, He has led me to study and pray so that I can understand and talk to others about what He did with me that morning. I have gone again and again to the Word of God to learn what transpired and how I could have been so deceived in my lost condition.

Over the years, God—in His love, mercy, and providence, and by the guidance of the Holy Spirit—has allowed me to see that there is a vast multitude of people who claim the name of Christ, as I did, but who in fact remain lost in their sins, living as what I call "unconverted believers." These are people who understand intellectually the gospel message, who believe they are saved, but whose hearts have not been truly changed from above.

God has called me to make every effort possible to warn these people of the reality of their condition. He has called me to provide directions for how "unconverted believers" can change their eternal destiny. In doing that, I want to be careful not to add unneeded burdens on those who are true believers but who are under Satan's attack of doubt over their salvation.

FOCUSING ON THE ONE TRUE GOD

As I studied the Bible, I began to understand how easy it was to religiously claim the name of Christ as my Savior, yet live in bondage to sin. I now comprehend why Jesus spoke so often about the religious zeal of the Pharisees, whose darkened hearts and minds remained lost to the truth of God. I learned that one of their worst errors was the consistent sin of their trivialization of God.

As I studied these things, I realized that I had been guilty of the same sins. I realized that the god I had served up to that time was not the God of the Bible but an idol I had fashioned and adopted from the examples of the lost souls around me who claimed to be believers. These people did not truly worship and serve the God of the Bible, but, like the Pharisees, practiced the sin of trivializing God.

My studies led me to see the great significance of God's beginning the Ten Commandments by addressing the foundational issue of idolatry. I believe He did that because how we view Him determines everything about us, and

God knew our minds would be the arena where much of the battle for our souls would be won or lost.

Sadly, too many who claim the name of Christ still disregard His commandments. Too many churches employ His name in all types of activities, programs, and approaches that focus more on the individual than on God. Many congregations emphasize "self-help" by way of self-renewal, a focus on wholeness, and the discovery of one's potential. Today, there is too much focus on self, which in many ways has become the greatest idol of all. If we are ever to be truly set free, we will need to depart from our preoccupation with ourselves and instead gaze outward toward the Almighty.

There is a wonderful New Testament account of an event that should help us understand our proper reaction to an encounter with the living God. The Bible tells us that just after the birth of Jesus Christ, wise men from the East followed a special star, understanding that it was a sign for the birth of a King. When they arrived at the site the star led them to, they entered the house where the Christ child lay. The Bible tells us that when they saw the baby Jesus, they fell on their faces and worshiped Him (Matthew 2:1–12).

What a message this brief encounter with Jesus sends! Let's pause to analyze what the Holy Spirit of God reveals in this passage. It is clear that these wise men had received some supernatural revelation that convinced them they should leave their homes and make a long, demanding journey to an unknown destination. They were being led to a foreign land in order to see that a very special King had been born. Stop and think about the obedience it required for them to leave their homes that way.

When these men arrived at the place where Jesus was,

they fell down and worshiped Him and presented Him with precious gifts. They had expected to find a King and had brought appropriate tokens of their adoration. They served Jesus with what they had. What a wonderful illustration of the importance of recognizing who God truly is!

In order to fully recognize the God of the Bible, we first need God's revelation, as these kings did. This is a special revelation that opens our eyes to Him and who He is, which comes through Scripture and the Holy Spirit. After we receive that revelation, we need to obediently follow Him where He leads us and bow and worship and serve Him with all we have. This is what it means to truly encounter the living God.

A few years ago, I saw a Christmas card that contained this statement: "Wise men still seek Him." It's a profound truth that those who are wise seek out the true God of the Bible. But I would add that all those who become wise will bow down and worship Him and serve Him with all they have to offer, because He is God.

He is, in fact, *the* sovereign God.

Two

AN AWARENESS OF EVIL

What comes out of a man is what makes him "unclean."
For from within, out of men's hearts, come evil thoughts,
sexual immorality, theft, murder, adultery, greed, malice,
deceit, lewdness, envy, slander, arrogance and folly. All
these evils come from inside and make a man "unclean."

— MARK 7:20–23 NIV

No evil is as displeasing to God or destructive to man but the evil of sin. Sin is worse than affliction, than death, than Devil, than Hell. Affliction is not so afflictive, death is not so deadly, the Devil not so devilish, Hell not so hellish as sin is. The four evils I have just named are truly terrible, and from all of them everyone is ready to say, Lord, deliver us! Yet none of these nor all of them together, are as bad as sin.

— RALPH VENNING

AN AWARENESS
OF EVIL

*W*hen I first came to salvation through Jesus Christ, God touched me with an awareness of the presence of evil in this world and its place in His ultimate plan.

Before my conversion, I knew evil existed. But frankly, the idea of evil seemed distant and not particularly relevant to me personally. Sure, there were times when I would join others in expressing indignation at some horrible event. I would be thankful that I was not like those who did that evil act. But for the most part, my preoccupation with my own existence left me little time to dwell on how evil impacted others.

All that changed when I first came to Christ. God began to open my eyes to the evil that was in me, around me, and in those close to me. Over the years since then, I have become keenly aware of the presence of evil in this world and in those who inhabit it.

The effects of evil are all around us. Evil resides in our marriages, in our families, and in our other relationships. It dwells in our communities and in all governments throughout the world. Evil lurks in the hearts of all people, awaiting an opportunity to make its play. It manifests itself in all areas of life, and it pollutes the things God meant for our good. It feeds the emotion of pride and leads us to exalt ourselves rather than God. It fosters selfishness, greed, and lust.

When evil isn't properly dealt with, it destroys everything it touches. The results of evil are undeniable. Horrible, indescribable things happen because of evil. It brings about the tragic consequences of death and destruction. All forms of violence, deception, deceit, corruption, and perversion are results of evil.

THE BEGINNING OF EVIL

The Bible helps us understand the root of evil and what a powerful force it can be. The Word tells us that evil came into the picture long before our present age. Long ago, in the heavens where God resides, a terrible event occurred, an event that has had profound consequences throughout history for God's creation and for all His creatures, including us. This event was Lucifer's rebellion against God.

Lucifer, whom we now call Satan, was one of God's archangels. We know that his pride—his own preoccupation with and love of himself—motivated him to rebel. Satan desired to be like God, and he was determined to use his great position to overthrow the Lord. This rebellion resulted in a great conflict that led to possibly one-third of God's angelic host siding with Satan in his rebellion.

God never desired that sin enter His wonderfully holy kingdom, nor did He want to see one of His highest-ranking angels rebel against Him. But the Lord was in control, and He permitted this rebellion to take place so that His eternal plan of redemption might be completed. This was so that the unsearchable riches of His grace might be revealed for all eternity. Looking at this from this perspective, it can be said that God allowed this event of rebellion to occur for His own purposes.

IT'S ALL PART OF HIS PLAN

The distinction between God's desires and His decrees in this context is very important, as it eases much of the confusion that has resulted from the misinterpretation or misapplication of certain Bible passages. We can see this side of God demonstrated in the life of the believer. God desires that we not sin; but we do sin, and He has decreed that our imperfection work for His ultimate purpose and for our ultimate sanctification. We do not fully understand how it all fits together, but I believe that when we get to heaven we will receive insight into how God used every event to contribute to the fulfillment of His marvelous plan.

God's account of the results of Satan's great rebellion provides us with many blessed truths, the most significant of which is the fact that it was all part of His plan. From eternity past, God knew and decreed that these events would occur. He is sovereign and controls the ultimate outcome of all things and events. It has been that way throughout history. God has never *caused* any evil to take place, but He *allows* evil and the horrors that follow it to take place and play their part in His master plan. Most important, since God is always in control, evil can only reach the level He allows.

As I've studied God's Word, I have learned that Satan is the ultimate cause and force behind evil. He is the ultimate example of self-worship and rebellion against God. I have also come to understand that Satan is cunning and deceptive in all his ways. He desires to destroy, to deceive, and to turn everything against God. Satan is the father of lies and of deception, and he continues to make war against

God and His kingdom. He presents himself as an angel of light, but his intent is purely evil.

At the same time, I have come to understand that Satan is God's Satan, and that he can only do what God permits him to do. Satan has great power, but He does not have the freedom many believe he has. He was God's creation, and, as it is with everything God has created, he operates within God's overall plan.

The book of Job provides some good insight on this subject. We see clearly in this account that God is actively involved in all aspects of His universe, including the lives of His people. We also see that God is firmly in control of the devil; Satan can do nothing God doesn't allow. God allowed the horrible events in Job's life for a purpose. We cannot fully understand these things, but we must resist the temptation to question God's actions. We must remember that He is God and that He makes no mistakes.

Satan's rebellion and his actions against Job demonstrate to us that nothing—not even the most profound act of evil—surprises God or takes place outside His ultimate plan. God knew from eternity past that Lucifer would rebel, and He knew the outcome of that rebellion.

God could have chosen to prevent the rebellion from occurring. He could have simply destroyed Satan at the moment he rebelled. But neither of these choices was part of His plan. Instead, God allowed the rebellion to take place, and He chose to permit Satan a restricted role in spreading his rebellion. Though we as human beings have very limited knowledge of how this spiritual war is being fought, we know that the Lord is allowing the war to continue.

And if we look closely at the Word of God, we can see

from the beginning of the war all the way to its ultimate outcome.

THE FALL AND
THE ULTIMATE VICTORY OVER EVIL

The Bible gives us a glimpse of how evil began, and it also explains how this evil first entered the human race. The book of Genesis tells us that Satan approached Eve in the garden and tempted her to question God's motivation and His supreme authority. The devil also tempted Eve by telling her that she would become like God—if she disobeyed in just one area. Eve allowed this temptation to conquer her, and she ate from the Tree of the Knowledge of Good and Evil, then tempted Adam with the fruit. When Adam ate of the fruit, sin entered into the human race because Adam had been made the representative of all mankind (1 Corinthians 15:22).

In this sense, Adam represented each of us there in the garden. In Adam, we were in a paradise with God. Everything we could ever want or need was there at our disposal. We lived in a state of innocence, free from the presence of sin—though not from the possibility of sin. We enjoyed daily fellowship with God, and we were at peace with Him, with ourselves, and with everything around us.

This all changed when we fell to Satan's temptation. When that powerful force of pride entered our hearts, we disobeyed God's clear orders, and we died spiritually. Evil entered the picture, and we lost our relationship with God.

It is only as we understand the fact that we are, by God's decree, *in* Adam that we can begin to comprehend the gravity of the fall of man. Most of the Bible deals with the story of what has occurred on our planet and how God continues to carry out His plan. That plan is to contrast good and evil, to allow everyone to see the consequences of evil, and to call unto Himself a people who will worship and serve Him for all eternity, free forever from any presence of evil.

God has controlled all of history and mankind—both the good and the evil deeds that have been done—in a way that has allowed His promised seed of redemption to come in the person of His Son, the Lord Jesus Christ. Through Him, God has provided the way for lost sinners to be redeemed from their sins and reconciled to Himself.

The Bible is the unfolding story of God's grace and mercy and how He overcomes the evil that brought about the fall of mankind. God has even revealed to us how He will finally deal with evil at the final judgment (Revelation 20).

On that day, each of us who have trusted in Jesus Christ for salvation will be completely free from all forms of evil. But now it is still part of our experience and our struggle.

Three

THE CONSEQUENCES OF SIN

As it is written: "There is none righteous, no, not one; there is none who understands; there is none who seeks after God. They have all turned aside; they have together become unprofitable; there is none who does good, no, not one. Their throat is an open tomb; with their tongues they have practiced deceit; the poison of asps is under their lips; whose mouth is full of cursing and bitterness. Their feet are swift to shed blood; destruction and misery are in their ways; and the way of peace they have not known. There is no fear of God before their eyes."

ROMANS 3:10–18 NKJV

We have no adequate idea of the dominion of sin, unless we conceive of it as extending to every part of the soul, and acknowledge that both the mind and heart of man have become utterly corrupt.

— JOHN CALVIN

THE CONSEQUENCES
OF SIN

$\mathcal{A}$ s a writer, I value the power of words to convey thoughts and ideas. The challenge for anyone trying to communicate an idea through words is to make the message clear and simple without oversimplifying it to the point that its original meaning is lost or altered.

It is amazing to me how thoughts and ideas can be so watered down because of the words used to convey them. A classic example of this centers around the very common farewell expression "good-bye." In the 1500s, the English used the phrase "May God by with ye" as a farewell, but by the 1600s, the expression had been shortened to "God by ye." Eventually it was shortened further to where it became "good-bye," the expression we use today. As you can see, most of the original meaning of the original phrase has been lost.

As I've studied the Bible over the years, I have become convinced that this is very similar to what has happened to how so many of us view God's words concerning our sin, the ultimate consequences of our sin, and how we can escape those consequences. Key passages from the Word are altered, abbreviated, or ignored to the point that great errors and misrepresentations of Scripture as it relates to sin and its consequences have become commonplace in many of our churches today.

I have come to the conclusion that this is no accident.

THE ORIGINAL SIN

One of Satan's most effective weapons against us is deception, and he uses it very effectively to encourage humans to question or overlook what God has to say in His Word about sin and the penalty for sin. Since God has communicated all we need to know about Him through the written Word, it makes sense that Satan would launch his greatest assault on this source of ultimate truth.

I believe that one of the greatest examples of this kind of deception deals with what the Bible refers to as "spiritual death." I pointed out in the last chapter that the consequences of Adam and Eve's disobedience to God's clear command not to eat from the Tree of the Knowledge of Good and Evil was death. This did not mean immediate physical death for the first couple, although the process of aging, which ultimately leads to physical death, began at that moment. Rather, it meant immediate spiritual death for both Adam and Eve.

As we read the account of the Fall, we can see the immediate impact of this spiritual death. Adam and Eve became aware of evil and were drawn to it. Soon, they realized they were naked and were ashamed. They had lost their innocence, and they both knew something was wrong, so in their distorted thinking, they hid from God. When God confronted them, they attempted to place blame on someone or something else—even on the Lord Himself—thinking they could avoid the consequences of their own decision.

This all happened because Adam and Eve took their eyes off of God and forgot His warning that the wages of sin would be death. They focused instead on the lies the devil had told them.

To this day, we can see this same pattern of sin playing itself out in the lives of people. They know evil and are attracted to it, and they commit evil acts. When they sin, they feel a sense of shame, which causes them to withdraw from any reminder of the true God of the Bible. They are also given to blaming other people or their own circumstances—or even God—for their sin, believing that they can avoid responsibility for what they have done.

The story of Adam and Even demonstrates to all of us the consequences of sin. They had enjoyed close personal fellowship with God, but because of their sin, they died spiritually and physically—just as God told them they would if they disobeyed. The Bible makes it clear that this condition was passed on to the entire human race through Adam, our representative.

ALL HAVE SINNED

The sad reality is that every person born since Adam and Eve is born spiritually dead and at enmity with God. This means that no one is born capable of knowing or responding to the triune God of the Bible, as we are all enemies of God. No person is born with the desire to respond to the Good News of the gospel or with a longing to know God better. This is a heart problem, because every person's heart is dead to the things of God.

A person may have interest in some forms of spirituality, but only to the point where it doesn't interfere with his or her freedom or comfort. Even most "religious" people are not interested in the true God or in His character, plans, or will. Rather, they are interested only in the blessings He gives them. In truth, they are only interested in fulfilling their own desires.

This is an area where Satan uses deception to fool his prey. Despite the fall of man, people have an awareness of God. Something inside them longs to enjoy God and have fellowship with Him. But at the same time, they have an awareness that something is not right within them, that something is missing. This is why so many religions and cults have come into existence. Man created religion to fill the void, but religion is always based on faulty or incomplete knowledge. Satan is only too pleased to present false religions and idol worship as a means to give humans some element of spiritual satisfaction. He will even allow people to get just close enough to the kingdom of God to feel that they know Him well enough to get to heaven. Sadly, though, they remain lost in their sin and under God's judgment.

People are not naturally drawn to the God of the Bible. They are not drawn to God's Son, the Lord Jesus Christ, or to the Holy Spirit of God. That is because everyone who lives in his or her natural state loves sin and hates the God of the Bible. The Bible tells us that everyone who hasn't been reborn spiritually is in fact a slave to his or her sin nature. The Bible also tells us that sin affects every part of the person.

These are the consequences of sin, and had God, through His Holy Spirit, not reached down to touch our hearts and minds, we would have remained lost.

FREEDOM FROM ABOVE

In and of ourselves, there is no little spark of the knowledge of God that can be kindled to a flame. Each person is born absolutely dead to God, and there is nothing that person can do to become spiritually alive. The only hope for true spiritual life is to be born again through an act of God that was planned before the world began.

My own life is an example of that hope in action.

As a child, I heard the gospel presented, heard Bible stories told, and felt the encouragement to ask Jesus Christ to come into my heart. I heard sermons on hell, and I heeded the warning that sinners will be tormented in that terrible place for ever and ever. So one Sunday, at the age of eight, I asked Jesus into my heart. From that moment on, I truly believed I was saved.

What was missing for me, however, was an action from the Holy Spirit. My decision left me with a sense that I was saved and on my way to heaven. I embraced the concept of "eternal security"—once saved always saved—in order to turn away the doubts I had about what had happened to me as a child. Intellectually, I could explain why I was sure I was going to heaven, but in reality I was just speaking what I knew to be the right words. I was still dead in my sins and on the broad road that leads to hell. Although I had an interest at times in spiritual things, they never altered my lifestyle to any great degree.

But one day, on a lonely road on the outskirts of Munich, Germany, I cried out to God, and in His wondrous grace and mercy, He reached down to me—a thirty-six-year-old man who had come to the end of himself, who was crushed and without hope—and brought me into His kingdom through a wonderful spiritual rebirth.

God the Holy Spirit had prepared me for that moment by beginning to create in me a new heart. This was the period of time when I came under the conviction of sin. I began to see how wrong my life was and how far off the mark I was. My life had not been centered on God, but on myself. As the Holy Spirit began to open my mind, I began to see that sin dominated every part of my life. This continued for a number of months, and my life got progressively worse. I was seeing all around me the consequences of my sin. But in the end, God, in His providence, brought me to a point of crying out for help. When I did, He was there.

I learned from that experience what Christ meant when He told Nicodemus that he must be "born again" in order to be saved, to truly escape the eternal consequences of sin (John 3:3). This means that we must be truly renewed by the power of Christ if we are to see God's kingdom. For too many years, I had neglected that part of the message.

God had to bring me to the end of myself by allowing the consequences of my sin to run their course. Thanks be to God that I was rescued and saved from my lost condition. Now I know that I won't suffer the eternal consequences of my sin, because Jesus has already paid the price for me.

Four

AN UNDERSTANDING OF BEING BORN AGAIN

Jesus replied, "I assure you, unless you are born again, you can never see the Kingdom of God. . . . The truth is, no one can enter the Kingdom of God without being born of water and the Spirit. Humans can reproduce only human life, but the Holy Spirit gives new life from heaven. So don't be surprised at my statement that you must be born again. Just as you can hear the wind but can't tell where it comes from or where it is going, so you can't explain how people are born of the Spirit."

JOHN 3:3, 5–8

This change of heart in a true Christian is so complete, that no word could be chosen more fitting to express it than the word, "regeneration," or "new birth." Doubtless it is no outward, bodily alteration, but undoubtedly it is an entire alteration of the inner man. It adds no new faculties to a man's mind, but it certainly gives an entirely new bent and bias to all his old ones. His will is so new, his tastes so new, his views of sin, the world, the Bible, and Christ so new, that he is to all intents and purposes a new man.

— J. C. RYLE

AN UNDERSTANDING
OF BEING BORN AGAIN

The expression "born again" is a familiar one in our culture, and it is very commonly used among Christians and even unbelievers. More than one recent United States president has made it a point to tell us he was born again. One of Billy Graham's many books is titled *How to Be Born Again*. And there are still places in the South where you will encounter road signs that state, "You Must Be Born Again."

As a child who attended church growing up in the South, I became quite familiar with the term "born again." I was taught from a very early age that being born again was absolutely essential to the salvation experience and that it came as a result of placing your faith in Jesus Christ as your personal Savior.

Over the past twenty years, I have learned that the act of placing your faith in Jesus Christ is not the sole element of true salvation and that it isn't even the first step in the process. I also have learned that the "new birth" is not a product of my faith in Christ, but rather the effect of what God does in my heart as He brings me to Himself.

I want to examine what it means to be truly "born again," and I'd like to start by talking about my own experience.

GETTING IT STRAIGHT

From the time I was a small child, I was taught that my act of embracing faith in Christ was the critical first step toward my new birth. I didn't understand much of the workings of true salvation; I just knew I wanted to do something to make sure I would go to heaven and, more important at the time, avoid going to hell.

I am still thankful that God in His providence allowed me to be exposed to strong warnings of the reality and the horror of hell. I remember thinking about the sermons I heard in which the preacher drove home the point that sinners will burn in hell forever. Frankly, these sermons on hell scared me, and I wanted to make sure I wasn't one of those who wound up there.

As I sat in church, I heard plenty about hell, but at the same time, I also heard about the Good News of the gospel of Jesus Christ. I heard the teaching that God loved me and gave His only Son, who came from heaven, became a man, took my sins on Himself, and died in my place. My earliest memories of my perceptions of God were of the wonder and beauty of the Lord Jesus Christ. I can honestly say that there was never a time when I doubted that there was a God in heaven. I also never doubted that God's Son was Jesus Christ and that He was the only way to heaven. In that respect, I was a believer.

There was no lack of teaching in my life about God and the things of God. I regularly attended an evangelical church, went to vacation Bible school, and left home for summer church camp. In addition to that, my public school started every day with prayer, and we studied the Bible regularly.

On one memorable Sunday when I was eight years old, some neighbors asked my parents if I could attend a Sunday night church service with them. These people were friends of the family, so my mother and father allowed me to go with them. The service turned out to be pivotal in my life, because at the end the preacher gave an altar call. I wanted very much to respond to the altar call, but I was too shy to walk forward in front of all those people. So I decided to respond to the call in my seat—quietly and privately. Right then and there, I prayed and asked Jesus into my heart.

From that evening on, I believed that because I had put my faith in Jesus Christ I was truly converted and "born again." I felt a great sense of relief from my fear of going to hell, and I was comfortable that if anyone asked, I could confidently state that I had been saved and was on my way to heaven.

Over the years, I have looked back at that event in my life as a genuine, heartfelt expression of faith. However, it was the expression of a heart that was still spiritually dead. For years, when I had doubts about my "walk with the Lord," I would go back to that time of decision and find assurance. However, through years of study, I have grown to understand that I lived twenty-eight years under the false belief that I had been converted and had become a child of God. But something was missing!

Now, I'm overjoyed to report that since my *true* conversion more than two decades ago, God the Holy Spirit has prompted and guided me as I studied what the Bible really says on the subject of being truly "born again."

STRAIGHT FROM THE SOURCE

In the gospel of John, one of the foundational books in the Bible on the topic of salvation, Jesus addresses the subject of the new birth. In chapter 3, Christ talks with a Pharisee by the name of Nicodemus about what it takes to see God's kingdom. Nicodemus acknowledges that God had sent Jesus and that He had come to teach. At that point, Jesus tells him, "I assure you, unless you are born again, you can never see the Kingdom of God" (verse 3).

Jesus' words about being born again were not a specific answer to any question from Nicodemus. Why did He begin the conversation with this statement? I believe Jesus said what He did because it is critical to understanding the process of true biblical salvation. In the original Greek language of this passage, the word *again* also carries with it the meaning "above." In other words, Jesus is telling Nicodemus that in order to see the kingdom of God, one must be born from *above*.

Nicodemus was confused at Jesus' words. He was a leader of the Jews and a devout Pharisee. The Pharisees were more or less the evangelicals of their day, and they had great knowledge of the Law and Jewish tradition. Yet Nicodemus couldn't quite grasp what the second person of the Trinity had told just him.

"What do you mean?" Nicodemus asked. "How can an old man go back into his mother's womb and be born again?"

I believe this question reveals something about Nicodemus's thinking, namely that he was trying to understand the supernatural and spiritual from the natural man's perspective. Consequently, he initially missed the truth Christ taught that day.

Christ responded to Nicodemus's question concerning being born again, explaining that "no one can enter the Kingdom of God without being born of water and the Spirit." There are numerous interpretations of the meaning of "water" in this verse, but I believe that it is used here to be emblematic of the Word of God. "Spirit" in this verse refers to the Holy Spirit, who moves on a person's heart, enabling him to receive saving faith. In other words, it is God's Word, illuminated by His Holy Spirit, that brings people to Christ.

The critical point of this exchange is when Jesus tells Nicodemus that the Holy Spirit gives new life from heaven. Using the illustration of the wind, which blows wherever it wishes, Jesus also makes it clear that God sovereignly bestows the new birth (John 3:6–8). Jesus points out that the Spirit moves where He determines, when He determines, and on whom He wills—and no human being can explain or duplicate the work of the Spirit.

DRAWN BY GOD

I think it is important to ask ourselves why Jesus used the analogy of birth to describe the process of coming to saving faith in Him. To better understand this analogy, it is helpful to ask some basic questions concerning our own physical birth: Did anyone ever have anything to do with his or her own conception? Do individuals ever have a say in who will be their parents? When they will be conceived? Where they will be born?

The answer to all these questions is a resounding no. Our natural birth is not within our control, and neither is our spiritual new birth. It is a gift from God, and we play no part in it. It is not our faith that produces the new birth, but the new birth that produces the kind of faith that enables us to respond to the gospel message. This produces genuine faith and repentance.

It is important that we understand that the new birth, which we also refer to as *regeneration,* is just one of the steps of salvation. God began His plan of salvation for fallen humanity in eternity past. He has brought it to pass by His design and for His purposes. He began this long before anything was created, and He will play out this plan for all of eternity.

Jesus' analogy of natural birth also fits because it provides us with an illustration of what takes place in both processes. For natural birth to occur, the ovum or egg must be fertilized with a sperm. This is the only combination that can produce life in the natural world. In the spiritual realm, which Christ was explaining to Nicodemus, it is necessary for God the Holy Spirit to plant within the heart the ovum of saving faith (Ephesians 2:8), which is then fertilized by the Word of God (1 Peter 1:23). The Word carries the power of divine life, and that life, when joined to the ovum of saving faith, forms a new creation. This is the new birth.

Now that we've discussed what the new birth *is,* let's examine what it looks like in the life of one who has truly been born again.

EVIDENCE OF THE NEW BIRTH

I have come to realize that my "salvation" experience as a child was of me and not of the Holy Spirit. You see, I naively tried to do myself what only God through His

Holy Spirit can do within me. What happened to me was, in fact, what I would call a "false conversion."

I now know that what happened to me that night was not a work of the Holy Spirit because it did not produce real faith and was void of biblical repentance—the understanding that I was a lost sinner and that I was at enmity with God. It also did not produce a transformed life.

My experience did not produce in me a broken and contrite heart, nor did it lead me to seek after God with all my heart and mind and soul and strength. Rather, it allowed me to remain comfortable in my pursuit of the things of this world and to serve myself and not my Creator. Another telltale sign that my conversion was not genuine was that I did not have a hunger for understanding of God's Word. Over the years, I tried to read the Bible because I knew I should, but with very little success. I prayed daily, but it was mostly ceremonial.

One of the most important things I have learned about true conversion is that when someone is truly "born again," there will be clear evidence of transformation. That person will never be the same and will never forget the fact that he or she has been transformed into a new creation. What God begins on the inside will eventually show up on the outside.

It is unfortunate that the term "born again" has become so broadly used and abused that it has lost its original meaning. It is often used in ways that do not reflect its biblical definition, and that has caused it to lose its true impact. As always, Satan does everything he can to bring confusion and deception to God's clear pronouncements. We need to recapture the true biblical meaning of "born again," and we need to be sure we understand it and can explain it to others. Most of all, we must be certain that we ourselves have truly been born again.

We should never forget the magnitude of the miracle that takes place when a lost sinner—one who is dead to spiritual truth—is made alive by the power of God. When a person has been born again from above, it initiates a truly life-changing process in the life of the "new creation."

Five

THE EXPERIENCE
OF TRUE CONVERSION

*Since you have heard all about him and have learned the
truth that is in Jesus, throw off your old evil nature and your
former way of life, which is rotten through and through, full
of lust and deception. Instead, there must be a spiritual
renewal of your thoughts and attitudes. You must display
a new nature because you are a new person,
created in God's likeness—righteous, holy, and true.*

EPHESIANS 4:21–24

Repentance, then, is the great, immediate, and pressing duty of all who hear the gospel. They are called upon to forsake their sins, and to return unto God through Jesus Christ. The neglect of this duty, is the rejection of salvation. Thus, of all the truths in the word of God, it may be said, that so far as they are believed in virtue of this spiritual apprehension, they will exert their appropriate influence upon the heart and consequently upon the life.

— CHARLES HODGE

THE EXPERIENCE
OF TRUE CONVERSION

*J*esus said in the third chapter of the gospel of John that we must be "born again" in order to see the kingdom of God. But He also stressed that we must be "converted" if we want to go to heaven.

In chapter 18 of Matthew's gospel, Christ answers the disciples' question about who would be the greatest in the kingdom of heaven by telling them that anyone who wants to see the kingdom must be "converted." He goes on to tell them what it means to be truly converted: "Assuredly, I say to you, unless you are converted and become as little children, you will by no means enter the kingdom of heaven. Therefore whoever humbles himself as this little child is the greatest in the kingdom of heaven" (Matthew 18:3–4 NKJV).

Jesus likens true conversion to childlikeness, which can be characterized by a spirit of simple trust and humility. We need to clearly understand this part of the salvation experience that Jesus referred to as "conversion." We must realize that true conversion follows the secret act of God that produces what we call the "new birth" in an unconverted person.

When someone is born again from God, he or she receives the capacity and the desire to respond in faith to the Good News of the gospel. This response constitutes the conversion Jesus spoke of. It represents the simple act of turning *from* sin—an act called "repentance"—and turning *to* Christ in faith. True conversion will always contain these two elements. It is impossible to have genuine faith and not forsake sin. Repentance and faith are like two sides of the same coin, the coin called true conversion.

Let's examine these two elements of true conversion, starting with repentance.

CALLED TO REPENTANCE

A quick look at a Bible concordance will show you that Scripture contains many, many calls to repentance. God commands each of us to repent because we all have gone our own way and chosen sin over Him. We have done that because we, in our fallen nature, are self-centered in all our ways.

Repentance is much more than feeling sorry for ourselves because we are suffering the consequences of our sin. It's more than regretting the circumstances that sin has brought. Repentance is not just our determination to change and do better.

True biblical repentance is a conscious act of the individual, and it results from a newly created spiritual awareness that affects the mind, the heart, and the will. Mentally, you become aware of your own sinfulness and the guilt that you sense before God. From your heart—the center of your consciousness, the emotional center of your being, and the part of you that forms your desires and affections—you realize what sin has done to you, to others, and, most of all, to God. You realize that sin and evil have been an integral part of every aspect of your life. From this understanding come true sorrow and regret for what you have done.

Last comes the change of the will. This is where what has occurred in the mind and heart impacts the way you live. Once you have truly comprehended the effect of your sin, it produces a godly sorrow and drives you to forsake sin and change your ways.

At this point, the Holy Spirit prompts us to seek out those we have sinned against—both God and those around us—and ask their forgiveness.

We need to realize that repentance is not a one-time exercise that occurs just at the moment of conversion. Repentance is an ongoing and necessary component of living out the Christian life on a daily basis. The initial repentance that takes place at the moment we are converted should establish a pattern of repentance that we will practice throughout our lives as believers. As we grow in our awareness of our own sinfulness—which we will when we are truly converted—we will see our continued need for repentance.

Now let's take a look at the other aspect of true conversion: faith.

CALLED TO FAITH

Faith is what we most commonly identify as being *the* mark of a true believer. Faith is simply putting one's trust in the person and work of Jesus Christ. Repentance is an act of turning from sin, and faith is the act of turning to Jesus. Faith is like repentance in that it involves changes in the mind, the heart, and the will.

With our minds we learn of God the Father, of His Son Jesus Christ, and of the Holy Spirit. We accept Their existence, even though we have not seen Them. With our minds we accept the Bible as what it declares itself to be, the infallible Word of God. We accept as fact that in the beginning God spoke everything into existence, that there was a fall from grace, and that all are sinners. We believe that God gave His Son as an atoning sacrifice for sin and that Jesus was crucified on a cross, died and was buried, and on the third day arose from the grave.

With our hearts, we determine to embrace and pursue what we have mentally accepted about God. With our will, we act on those things as we allow them to take root in our daily actions. We rest in and respond to the person of Jesus Christ and resist the human tendency to depend on ourselves.

True faith involves commitment and action, and not just the mental assent and emotion we commonly associate with faith. This is what the Bible means by the term "saving faith."

Many people who intellectually accept biblical truths have no problem claiming the name "Christian" for themselves. But many of those people have not determined in their hearts to make those truths the guiding force in their lives. This is an incomplete faith, a faith that is not the result of a true conversion.

PICTURES OF AUTHENTIC CONVERSION

We can see a wonderful example of true conversion in the account of the thief on the cross. We have no reason to believe that this criminal had any prior knowledge of Jesus or who He claimed to be. Yet, in the end this thief had been truly converted.

The gospel of Matthew tells us that two thieves were crucified with Jesus, one on His right and one on His left (Matthew 27:38). At first, both thieves joined with the crowd in ridiculing and mocking Jesus: "Even the robbers who were crucified with Him reviled Him with the same thing" (verse 44 NKJV). Both robbers started this experience as lost sinners, dead to anything spiritual.

But Luke 23:39–42 tells us that only one of the robbers continued to mock Jesus, while the other underwent a dramatic heart change. This repentant criminal, who was dying for his wrongdoing, recognized God and His right to judge those who do evil. He accepted the sentence due him for his crimes, and he also turned in faith to ask Christ to remember him in His kingdom.

There are also nonbiblical examples of "religious" people finding true salvation.

John Wesley's conversion story demonstrates so well how someone can be what I call an "unconverted believer." In his early years, Wesley appeared strong in his faith and was active in ministry, yet he wasn't truly converted. He grew up in a strong Christian home and received a Bible-centered education. Later, he became a great Bible scholar and was active in promoting the gospel. But the gospel had never touched his life in a personal way.

Wesley traveled to America to work as a missionary to American Indians, but the story goes that as he was returning to England, he observed a group of Moravian believers who were fearless in the face of a terrible storm. Wesley realized that he lacked something they had. He realized that he was not truly converted. After his return to England, Wesley attended a Sunday service at a small assembly on Aldersgate Street. It was there that God met Wesley. That day, he was truly converted.

MY OWN CONVERSION

I wrote earlier that my conversion was truly a "Damascus Road" experience—like that of the apostle Paul when Jesus struck him down on the road to Damascus. My life was marked from that time forward. I knew I'd had an encounter with God when, in a brief moment in the early hours of that October morning, I came to the end of myself and cried out, "God, please help me!" In an instant, a great peace overshadowed the anguish I'd felt.

I immediately sensed God's love and a new sense of reality I had never known. None of my life's circumstances had changed, yet everything about me was different. Everything I processed mentally took on new meaning. Something was happening, something I was not yet able to fully grasp. Within a short time I realized what had happened: I had been converted. I was overcome with a mixture of great joy in my encounter with the Lord and great sadness at the recognition of my own sinfulness.

I was soon overwhelmed with a sense of fear as I began to realize that until that morning I had been a lost sinner on my way to hell—all the while deceiving myself into believing that I was on my way to heaven. I looked back on my past life, and I saw an ugly picture. I realized that I had been a captive to sin.

Over the following months, I came face-to-face with the import of the consequences of sin that, at times, seemed unbearable. But God, in His grace and with His tender mercies, sustained me. My life took on a different dimension in many ways. I was immediately burdened for those who were yet to be converted as I had been. I struggled with tears as I looked out my office window at the city of

Munich, West Germany, and thought about the thousands of people there who were lost without Christ.

From the very first morning after I was converted, I went to the Bible and began to truly understand what it said. It was as though my eyes had been opened for the very first time. I was deeply moved by what I read in the Word, and I wondered how I could have been so blinded for so many years.

I realized that I had been dead to spiritual things even though I had been alive physically. I have never stopped praising God for His gift of true conversion.

NEW SIGHT

Some years ago I read about an incident in the life of Helen Keller. Something took place that transformed her life, and she wrote about it in her autobiography. This passage illustrates what happened to me on that special day of my conversion:

> We walked down the path to the well-house, attracted by the fragrance of the honeysuckle with which it was covered. Someone was drawing water and my teacher placed my hand under the spout. As the cool stream gushed over one hand she spelled into the other the word water, first slowly, then rapidly. I stood still, my whole attention fixed upon the motions of her fingers. Suddenly I felt a misty consciousness as of something forgotten—a thrill of returning thought; and somehow the mystery of language was revealed to me. I knew then that "w-a-t-e-r" meant the wonderful cool something that was flowing over my hand, that living word awakened my soul, gave it light, hope, joy, set it free. There

were barriers still, it is true, but barriers that could in time be swept away. I left the well-house eager to learn. Everything had a name, and each name gave birth to a new thought. As we returned to the house, every object which I touched seemed to quiver with life. That was because I saw everything with the strange, new sight that had come to me.[1]

My conversion was like that. It was as though God had turned on the light of my mind so that I could, for the first time, see and understand what He had provided in this unique Book called the Bible. For days, I found it hard to put the Bible down. I was like someone who had just discovered how to eat. I didn't want to stop consuming God's Word.

God also shed light on my sinfulness. As a child, I had learned to admit my sins, but after my conversion I was for the first time truly conscious of my own iniquity. I had always had a realization of the sin that was around me, but for the first time in my life, I was developing within me a hatred of sin.

These were the evidences of true conversion in my life. They were the proof that something awesome had taken place within me, something that ensured that I'd never be the same.

As I look back on the time since I first came to know Jesus Christ as my Lord and Savior, I can gratefully say that He continues to show me the evidence in my life of true conversion.

NOTE

1. Helen Keller, *The Story of My Life* (New York: Houghton Mifflin, 1928), 23–24.

Six

AN AWARENESS
OF TRUTH

*The law of the Lord is perfect, converting the soul; the
testimony of the Lord is sure, making wise the simple; the
statutes of the Lord are right, rejoicing the heart; the
commandment of the Lord is pure, enlightening the eyes;
the fear of the Lord is clean, enduring forever; the
judgments of the Lord are true and righteous altogether.*

— PSALM 19:7–9 NKJV

The foundation of all true knowledge of God must
be a clear mental apprehension of His perfections as
revealed in Holy Scripture. An unknown God can
neither be trusted, served, nor worshipped.

— ARTHUR W. PINK

AN AWARENESS
OF TRUTH

*O*ne of the most important things I have learned in my twenty-plus years as a believer is that God has provided us truth and wisdom through His written Word, the Bible. I have come to see that the Bible is the true Book of life, and that it helps believers grow in their understanding about God and His relationship to all of life's circumstances. I have learned that the Word of God is sufficient for dealing with every issue, problem, and consequence we face.

We can learn from the Bible how to better comprehend the things God has revealed about Himself, about His wonderful plan of redemption, and about how salvation has been made possible through the God-man, Jesus Christ. The Bible also provides clear instruction on how we as believers should live. It tells us that our major focus in life is to be conformed to the image of our Lord, to become holy as our Father in heaven is holy. The Word also gives us specific warnings and instructions on how to avoid falling into sin, the behavior that keeps us from being the "salt and light" that the world desperately needs us to be.

Finally, I've come to realize how critical the truth of the Word of God is in leading people to saving faith in Jesus Christ. Vast numbers of people come to Christ by simply reading the Word of God and being quickened by the Holy Spirit. The Bible contains the truth of God that sets people free from the bondage of sin and puts them on a path to the kingdom of God.

When you look at the truth the Word of God gives His people, is it any wonder that our enemy, Satan, has challenged it from the very beginning?

AN ASSAULT ON THE TRUTH

Satan has always tried to distract people from the Word because he doesn't want us to know the truth the Bible communicates to us. If you were to study the history of the Bible and how people have treated it over the past millennium, you would see the numerous—and oftentimes effective—ways Satan has attempted to discredit and even destroy it.

I believe that the acceptance of and commitment to biblical truth today has been so eroded that our time can be compared to the time immediately before the Reformation, when the Bible was not available or accessible to the vast majority of the population. The problem today is not of accessibility to the Word but of commitment to it. Sadly, multitudes of professing Christians have so abandoned the reading and study of the Bible that it has been rendered almost irrelevant in their lives. Many still hold the Bible as an esteemed symbol of their faith, yet they live their lives as though it didn't exist. Many people say they believe the Bible, but they have no idea what it really says or how to seriously read and study it.

An extraordinary number of quality resources are available today to help us read, study, and understand the Bible. Still, with all the help available to us, a growing number of professing believers invest little or no time in the pursuit of scriptural truth. I believe that a majority of those who claim the name of Christ fall into a category I call "biblically illiterate."

Fewer and fewer people in our day accept the Bible as the final authority on matters that affect their daily lives. Though many accept the Word of God as inerrant, they often question its sufficiency to address all the issues they face. They then turn to non-biblical solutions. When they do that, their focus is drawn further away from the ultimate source of truth, which is the Word of God. This is one of the ways the world gains influence within the church. If that trend continues, the church will eventually be no different from the world it is called to confront and change.

The modern church is not unlike the children of Israel, who enjoyed close fellowship with the triune God as they worshiped, first in the tabernacle and then in the temple. Yet over time, they came to take this communion for granted, and ultimately the presence of God left their temple for good. Today, many true believers have gradually gotten away from a regular reading and study of God's Word. I believe this grieves the Holy Spirit, and I believe those who have fallen into that trap are in need of repentance.

I've learned some important lessons about the subject of truth, and I hope they will add some perspective to this subject.

BARRIERS FROM THE TRUTH

In the 1950s, when I was growing up, many if not most people held the Bible as the standard of all truth. During that time, I was exposed to the Bible through many different means, including the printed Bible and biblical preaching at church and over the radio. I also had a chance to see the truth of the Word modeled in the lives of people around me. I am thankful that I had the exposure to the Word that I did. I am convinced that this exposure to the Bible had a restraining influence in my life and that it reminded me of the standards of living that God has set for His people.

However, in the fifty-plus years I have walked this earth, I have witnessed the disastrous consequences—in my own life, in the lives of others, and in our society—of exchanging God's wisdom for that of man. I have seen that when we reduce or eliminate God's influence in our own lives, we will suffer, and that is exactly what happened to me. Even though I had every opportunity as a youth to follow God, I chose to follow man. Like so many of my generation, my idol was the god of prosperity. I was focused on success and wealth and not on God.

I learned personally the folly of idolatry, of pursuing my own way rather than pursuing God. I learned that Satan uses these "false gods" to lead me and others away from the true God of the Bible. I learned that allowing God's influence in our lives to be reduced eventually affects our marriages, our families, our friendships, our communities, and ultimately our nation.

I believe there are two major barriers to believers' pursuit of biblical truth. The first barrier—and one I referred to in my preface—is the lack of true conversion in many believers' lives. These are people who have a form of godliness but in reality they deny the power of God's Word and God's ways (2 Timothy 3:5). Because they claim the name of Christ but live lives that mirror those of the world, the power that should be visible to a lost world is absent. In addition, these individuals have little interest in the truth of the Bible.

Until someone is truly born again he or she cannot fully comprehend the truth. God's truth as revealed in the Bible must be spiritually discerned with the guidance of the Holy Spirit. Just as it is possible to know a great deal *about* God and yet not know Him in a way that brings salvation, it is also possible to know the Bible intellectually but miss the message that leads to salvation.

A person who is not truly converted lacks the capacity to grasp and understand the truth of the Bible. This person can't fully understand what God has revealed about Himself, about who we are, and about what separated us from Him. That is because the Spirit of God has not opened his heart and mind to the truth of God's Word.

The second barrier to biblical truth for believers is the preoccupation with things that take up their time and keep them from spending time in the Word. This also happens within the walls of churches that don't focus enough on the expository preaching of the Bible or on the necessity of accepting it as the final authority over our lives. Sadly, many churches have replaced sound study of the Scriptures with all types of expression and entertainment. Even more tragic is the fact that many churches have begun to question some of the foundational truths of the faith.

When we neglect the truth of God as He has revealed it in the Scriptures, it is only a matter of time before we fall prey to Satan and his temptations. When that happens, we soon find ourselves out of fellowship with the Lord, ineffective for Him, and miserable.

GOD'S WORD: TRUSTWORTHY AND TRUE

The last four chapters of the book of Revelation introduce us to the culmination of what God planned before the beginning of time. This passage also has something to tell us about God's spoken and written Word.

Chapter 19 begins with an account of vast crowds shouting, "Hallelujah! Salvation is from our God. Glory and power belong to him alone. His judgments are *just and true.* . . . Hallelujah! For the Lord our God, the Almighty, reigns. Let us be glad and rejoice and honor him. For the time has come for the wedding feast of the Lamb, and the bride has prepared herself " (verses 1–2, 6–7, italics added). Then the angel who was standing with the apostle John said to him, "Blessed are those who are invited to the wedding feast of the Lamb. . . . *These are true words* that come from God" (verse 9).

Verse 11 states, "Then I saw heaven opened, and a white horse was standing there. And the one sitting on the horse was named *Faithful and True.*" Moving on to verse 5 of chapter 21, we read, "And the one sitting on the throne said, 'Look, I am making all things new!' And then he said to me, 'Write this down, for what I tell you is *trustworthy and true.*'"

Finally in Revelation 22:6, we read, "Then the angel said to me, 'These words are *trustworthy and true:* "The Lord God, who tells his prophets what the future holds, has sent his angel to tell you what will happen soon."'"

It is extremely interesting and telling how much emphasis God the Holy Spirit places on "truth" in this passage. In one way, this is the culmination of an emphasis throughout the Bible on His truthfulness and faithfulness. One aspect of that truth is the fact that the God of the Bible is the true and only God and that all other gods are only idols.

Another aspect of God's truthfulness is the fact that *all* His words and thoughts are truthful and trustworthy, and that includes His written Word, the Bible. In the final analysis, *He* is the final standard of truth.

Seven

BECOMING
A NEW CREATION

Those who become Christians become new persons. They are not the same anymore, for the old life is gone. A new life has begun! All this newness of life is from God, who brought us back to himself through what Christ did. And God has given us the task of reconciling people to him. For God was in Christ, reconciling the world to himself, no longer counting people's sins against them. This is the wonderful message he has given us to tell others.

2 CORINTHIANS 5:17–19

To be a Christian is no light matter. It is a call to a transformed life and to perseverance through whatever troubles may arise. It may be the hardest thing anyone can do. Yet anyone can do it, with Christ supplying the necessary strength. In the end it is the only thing that really matters.

— JAMES MONTGOMERY BOICE

BECOMING
A NEW CREATION

$\mathcal{M}$y wife and I recently completed a very special trip to Munich, Germany, where twenty years earlier God met us and, through His Holy Spirit, produced in us the supernatural transformation of the new birth. That encounter two decades ago was when we were truly converted, when we received God's gift of saving faith and repentance.

Our visit to Munich was a cherished homecoming, and it evoked deep emotions within each of us as we commemorated that monumental turning point in our lives. We were reminded of how profoundly altered our lives had been and how God had literally changed who and what we were to become. We remembered how we had by God's power become new creations and how we had been set on a new life journey that will not be complete until we arrive in heaven.

My wife and I had both seen in our own lives the resurrection power of God. We had been dead in our sins and trespasses but were delivered to the newness of life found only in a personal relationship with the Lord Jesus Christ. Each of us had been called by name from our tomb of sin: "Mary, come forth!" God called out. "Bill, come forth!"

My wife and I had spent most of our lives as professing Christians, so the impact of finally coming to a true saving faith in Jesus turned our entire world upside down. Up to that point, the whole foundation of our lives was crumbling around us, and we had nowhere to run but to God. We had come face-to-face with the reality of who we had been and who we were becoming.

From the time of our conversion forward, the hand of God has been shaping us in more ways than I can count. We still do not understand all that God has initiated in our lives, but we know this: The changes God has made and is making in us are transforming us into new creatures.

A NEW WAY OF LIFE

The most dramatic change that took place in my life that morning in Munich was that my eyes were opened to the truth of the Bible. I can remember how a number of passages I had read so many times suddenly became crystal clear. I was astounded at the impact God's Word had on me after that. For example, as I read the first chapter of Romans, I didn't just comprehend it but was in full agreement with it and began to apply it to my own life. I read about His anger against sin—my sin. I read and realized that recognition of God's truth is built into our consciences, yet we—I—want to refuse to worship Him as God, that our minds become dark and confused when we reject Him.

Within days of my conversion, I changed my whole approach to life. Before, I had been driven by my own agenda—my career and the accumulation of things. After that, though, I began asking God to help me order my life according to His priorities and for His glory. God had so totally changed my outlook that going to Him this way was easy for me. I felt His overwhelming presence in my life in those early weeks of being a new creation. The love He poured out on me motivated me to do everything I could to please Him. That meant searching His Word for truth.

The truth of God's Word gave me the strength and desire to immediately change my worldly habits. The desire and attraction I had felt for those things for so many years left me and were replaced with new desires that reflected God's commandments for me. The Holy Spirit began to lead and teach me, and He also convicted me of my need to continue to repent and forsake sinful habits and attitudes.

God was doing great things in me, and He was also doing great things in my family—particularly in my wife, who was being made a new person before my very eyes.

A NEW FAMILY

I am thankful to God for the extraordinary mercy He showed in saving me and my wife within days of each other. I still believe that God ordered the circumstances in such a way that we would need to be completely dependent on Him and His Word during this time in our lives. In addition, He ordered the circumstances so that we would be forced to cling to each other and to "work out [our] salvation with fear and trembling" (Philippians 2:12 NIV).

Our first few months of new life in Christ were punctuated by an awareness of the devastating cost of sin in our lives and in our marriage. God the Holy Spirit used the impending breakup of our relationship to bring each of us to the end of self and to force us to cry out to Him for help. It was then that God brought us to true repentance and faith, which led us to become new creations in Christ.

God began a great work in our lives and in our marriage, and He began convicting us of areas where we needed change. One of the first areas He pointed out was how we had failed our children as parents. Though we had taken them to church and taught them right from wrong, we had not nurtured them in Christ. Our love for our children was not a selfless love. They also saw contradictions in our lives, as we too often said one thing and did another. As the Holy Spirit ministered to us, we began to recognize areas of sin we needed to confess and ask forgiveness for. God also prompted us to explain to our children what He had just done in our lives. From that time on, we asked for the Lord's help in being better parents and showing our children Christ.

God also brought me under conviction concerning my attitudes and actions toward my parents. I held a great deal of bitterness toward my mother and father concerning some decisions that had serious consequences for me. I realized I hadn't loved and respected my parents as the Bible has clearly commanded me to do. God was teaching me that my responsibility is to deal with my sins and let Him deal with the sins of others, even those sins committed against me. I wrote my mother and father a letter accepting responsibility for my sins and asking them for their forgiveness.

A NEW AWARENESS

During those early months of our new lives in Christ, my wife and I both began to receive new understanding, as God opened our eyes to His reality.

Both of us had good head knowledge of what the Bible said. But after our conversion, we began to have a clearer spiritual understanding of the meaning of the Word. It was as if God turned on the lights for us and allowed us, for the first time, to see who and what we truly were before a holy and righteous God. He showed us through His Word how far we had been from Him and how we had been living in the false security of our own self-righteousness. He revealed the awesomeness of what He had done for us when He saved us. Each day brought a new awareness of His grace, mercy, and patience, and of how important those things were as we struggled to conform to our new calling as children of God.

Another aspect of our becoming a new creation in Christ was an awareness on our part of the spiritual deadness of those around us. We realized that most of the people around us—our family, our friends, and others—were without Christ. We both felt a great burden for the lost. Shortly after our conversion, we would spend time just sitting on a bench in the city of Munich weeping and praying for those around us who didn't know or weren't interested in the God of our salvation. We prayed that God would enable us to tell others what had just happened to us.

We began telling our testimony, and within a few weeks we saw God bring a couple who were our friends to a saving faith in Jesus Christ. We also observed God beginning a work in the life of our daughter, who came to saving faith within a few weeks after we told her what had happened to us. Looking back, we can now clearly see that God initiated a moving of the Holy Spirit, which brought salvation in the lives of a few lost sinners we knew. We also saw the power of lovingly speaking the truth to others and of sharing what God had done in the lives of two redeemed sinners.

All this happened because God moved on us and made us new creations in Him.

THE REAL THING

True salvation comes from God. It is produced when He pours out the power of the Holy Spirit. This brings spiritual rebirth to dead people and leads to conversion through true repentance and faith in the Lord Jesus Christ.

When people are born again and converted, they become new creations. The transformation God begins in them at the moment they are saved is by no means complete, but the evidence of what has taken place in them begins to surface for the world to see. God works differently in each person, but one thing is a constant for those who have truly been converted: They will never be the same.

Thinking of this reminds me of something I read from a devotional by one of the great preachers of the past, Charles H. Spurgeon. He wrote:

> Regeneration is a subject which lies at the very basis of salvation, and we should be very diligent to take heed that we really are "born again," for there are many who fancy they are, who are not. This great work is supernatural. It is not an operation which a man performs for himself: a new principle is infused, which works in the heart, renews the soul, and affects the entire man. To wash and dress a corpse is a far different thing from making it alive: man can do the one, God alone can do the other.[1]

Since the time of the Fall, man has been preoccupied with "dressing the corpse"—all the while tragically missing the truth of the need to become a new creation by the supernatural work of God.

We should each pause and ask ourselves these vital questions:

- Have I really been guilty of just trying to "dress a corpse" rather than falling on my face and seeking God's help?
- What are the real priorities of my life? What am I really striving for?
- Where is God in all my activities and in my daily planning?
- What are the true, deep desires of my heart?

What we say we believe has no real meaning. Rather, it's how we live that bears testimony that we are a new creation, that we have been raised from spiritual death to spiritual life.

Each of God's new creations will progress and change at different rates and in different ways. Some, by His grace, grow quickly, make fewer mistakes, and "stumble" less on their way to transformation. Some struggle and seem to make very little progress, and others start strong only to go astray, then have to almost start over. Many will remain babes in the faith because they fail to make use of all that God has provided for them to grow.

But all who have been born again and converted will bear evidence in their lives of being new creations. There will be differences in their lives, for those God calls He also sanctifies. When God calls you by name, you will go from death to life and you will be changed forever.

I would encourage you to take the time to examine your life to see that you truly are a new creation in Christ. Ask God to help you to look honestly at who you truly are in His eyes. After all, if you are planning on going to heaven, it is who you are in *His* eyes that will matter. I have learned that we can be blinded to who we are and live completely unaware of our desperate need to be made a new creation.

So, examine your life, then ask yourself, "Am I truly a new creation?"

NOTE

1. Charles H. Spurgeon, *Morning and Evening* (Peabody, Mass.: Hendrickson, 1995), March 6 morning entry, "You Must Be Born Again."

Eight

WAITING
ON GOD'S TIMING

*Have you not known? Have you not heard? The everlasting
God, the Lord, the Creator of the ends of the earth, neither
faints nor is weary. His understanding is unsearchable. He
gives power to the weak, and to those who have no might He
increases strength. Even the youths shall faint and be
weary, and the young men shall utterly fall, but those who
wait on the Lord shall renew their strength; they shall
mount up with wings like eagles, they shall run and
not be weary, they shall walk and not faint.*

— ISAIAH 40:28–31 NKJV

God is not in a hurry. He is a patient craftsman as he shapes lives into the image of his Son. He is prepared to wait. He knows there is all eternity for the finished item to be enjoyed. You and I must likewise turn aside from instant methods to knowing the will of God in the long term.

— SINCLAIR B. FERGUSON

WAITING
ON GOD'S TIMING

*M*ost of us are familiar with the expression "Timing is everything." History contains many examples of the importance of timing, two of which proved to be turning points in World War II.

The first example of the importance of timing took place December 7, 1941, when the Empire of Japan launched a surprise attack on Pearl Harbor. The primary objective of the raid was to destroy the United States naval fleet, giving the Japanese forces control of the Pacific Ocean. Japan would likely have succeeded in accomplishing its goal, except that the prize targets of the fleet—three aircraft carriers —were out at sea on maneuvers that day. Had the timing been different, had those carriers been in the harbor with the other ships, the course of the war would have been drastically altered.

Another World War II example of the importance of timing took place in June of 1944, when the Allied Forces, under General Eisenhower, launched the greatest military invasion in history on the shores of France. This was the famous "D-Day" landing, which the Allies hoped would lead to the recapture of Europe from the Nazi forces. The invasion, though it cost thousands of young lives, was a success. History now tells us that timing was a vital element in the invasion, as Hitler's delay in sending reinforcements was probably the single most significant factor in the Allied victory. Had the German leader sent more men, the Allied forces may have been faced with even more devastating casualties and likely failure in the invasion.

Timing is a vital factor not just in military history, but in business, sports, relationships, and every other avenue of life. Timing is a huge part of the Christian life as well, and one of the most important things I've learned from God's Word is that He orders the events of time and that He is Lord of time and Lord over all circumstances.

GETTING AHEAD OF GOD

God is sovereign over all the affairs of our lives, including the minor details. He never makes any mistakes, and there is no such thing as luck or coincidence. When He allows something to take place in our lives, we can be assured that His timing is perfect. No person or event is beyond God's control.

The Bible makes it clear that no event is beyond God's control, but the Word also tells us that we are responsible for our choices and that there are consequences for those choices. This is one of the great paradoxes of Scripture. As finite creatures, we cannot comprehend how God can be in control over all events yet at the same time we are allowed to make choices for which we will be held responsible. This is one of many areas where we must submit to God's revealed truth and accept it by faith, knowing that nothing is beyond His ability to execute.

One of the sinful choices many Christians make today is failing to acknowledge God's rightful place as they plan the course of their lives. Many believers act and think presumptuously in that they lose sight of the facts that God is sovereign and that nothing happens outside His control. God's people also sin when they become impatient, thinking they know better than God the right course of action for their lives. They proceed on that path, which is different from the one God charted for them. They look to their own wisdom rather than God's wisdom.

Christians often move forward with their own plans, even though they lack the biblical knowledge they need to help them ascertain God's plan. But the Bible tells us that at the appropriate time God will bless us and give us wisdom and the answers we need—*if* we wait on Him for those things. This is why the reading and the study of God's Word is so important. Without this discipline, it is impossible to know God's will, much less allow that will to guide us.

BIBLICAL CONSEQUENCES
OF NOT WAITING

God has perfect knowledge and knows the end from the beginning, so He is never in a hurry. He knows just the right timing in bringing His will to pass. Sadly, we fallen humans often have a tough time waiting on that timing.

There are numerous examples in the Bible of God's own people falling into the trap of impatience, acting presumptuously, taking matters into their own hands, and moving out ahead of God. Included in these stories are the consequences of His people falling into that sin.

In the book of Exodus, we read the account of Moses taking it upon himself to try to avenge the cruelty of the Egyptians toward God's people, the children of Israel. Moses, the man God chose to lead the people out of slavery and into the Promised Land, lashed out in anger and killed one of his people's oppressors. Moses acted outside of God's perfect will and timing, and he had to flee for his life. In this account we see an example of how God, in His providence, uses even our own mistakes for our good and for His glory. God used Moses' disobedience to bring about His will. God's plan was for Moses to spend forty years in the desert preparing to lead the rescue and eventual Exodus of His people from Egypt to the land He had promised Abraham.

Another biblical example of someone failing to wait on God was one of the patriarchs, Jacob. Because God had revealed before Jacob and Esau's birth that the descendants of the younger would rule over the descendants of the older, there had developed a strong element of envy in Jacob toward his brother Esau. At one point, Jacob tricked Esau into selling his birthright to him, and on another occasion he tricked his father, Isaac, into giving him the blessing that was intended for Esau. Because these acts were not within God's perfect will and timing, Jacob had to flee from his home and from the anger of his brother. In order to teach Jacob to wait on Him, God eventually allowed him to become the victim of some of his uncle's tricks (Genesis 31:7).

Perhaps the most dramatic biblical example of someone failing to wait on the Lord is the story of King Saul. His disobedience in not waiting on God's prophet Samuel to make a burnt offering on behalf of the armies of Israel resulted in God's removal of His blessing from Saul. Saul's patience ran out when Samuel did not come at the intended time and Saul sacrificed the offering himself, which was strictly forbidden in the Law. Samuel informed Saul that had he been faithful to God's command, his kingdom would have been established forever over Israel. Because of his disobedience, however, Saul's dynasty would come to an end (1 Samuel 15:28).

These stories should remind us that God's ways are not like our ways and that His timing is perfect. God always operates with complete knowledge, whereas we are limited in what we know. The more we grow in our knowledge and understanding of our awesome God, the easier it becomes for us to learn to wait on His direction and His timing.

LEARNING TO WAIT

Over the years since I first came to true salvation, I have observed how natural and comfortable it is for godly, mature believers to wait on the Lord. I believe that is because they have learned, over time, the blessing and comfort that comes with waiting on God's perfect timing.

I've learned these things myself. I wrote earlier that in many ways I have been writing this book for twenty years. But in another way, this book marks the beginning of a new chapter in my life. That chapter is the fulfillment of something God put on my heart just after I came to saving faith in Christ.

As my wife and I began to tell others what God had done in our lives, we witnessed the transforming power of God in a couple who were friends of ours. We soon saw them come to a saving faith in Christ. After that happened, we sensed a genuine stirring of the Holy Spirit, and I believed God was calling me to prepare to become an evangelist.

During those early months after my conversion, the presence of God was near and powerful in my life, and it seemed only natural that God would call me to become an evangelist. I believed God had shown me very clearly His plans for my future. I truly believed that God wanted me to be an evangelist so that I could be part of a huge movement and outpouring of the Holy Spirit, like the one I had been witnessing on a small scale. I was excited. I had built my business career on my ability to communicate clearly and persuasively, so full-time evangelism seemed like a logical and natural fit for me. This sense of calling helped lead me to resign from the position that had taken me to Germany.

I had come in contact with another believer who encouraged me to think seriously about attending a Bible school in order to help me build a solid foundation on which to build my career as an evangelist. In an example of God's providence, I moved our family to upstate New York, where I began preparing for my new course of life. The move provided us with loving support and encouragement, as well as an introduction to a whole new world of living by faith.

As time passed, it became obvious that what I had thought was God's call wasn't materializing. My initial excitement at what I believed was a call to evangelism began to wane as doors closed for me. Several events in my life brought me to a point of wondering what God's plan for me really was. I wondered how I could have been so wrong about my calling during those early months after my conversion.

After one semester of Bible school, the scheduling didn't work out, and I felt a leading to move back south to North Carolina. I was sure that God would make it clear to me where He wanted me to go and how He was going to use me.

As it turned out, I waited two more years before God led me to begin work to open a Christian bookstore. Little did I know at that point that this was just the beginning of my entry into Christian publishing and that God would eventually lead me to join Moody Press.

LEARNING FROM HINDSIGHT

Looking back at twenty years of faith, I can see clearly the truth that God never makes mistakes and that His timing is always perfect. I've made plenty of mistakes, but, in His providence, He used my sins and errors to move me toward His purposes and plans. I take great joy in my calling to Christian publishing. I feel greatly privileged to have the opportunity to be a published author so that I can teach and encourage others on some of the basics of being a true believer in Christ.

I truly sense that with the writing of this book, my original calling to be an evangelist has begun to be fulfilled. That calling is being fulfilled, not in the way that I had first thought, but in a way I couldn't have imagined all those years ago: by writing a book in which I communicate the marvelous story of God's way of salvation, which He has made known in the Bible.

I am now certain that it was God's plan all along for me during the past twenty years to read and meditate on His Word, study what others have written on the subject of salvation, and continuously ask God to show me the truth.

God knew I would need twenty years of refining and preparation before He opened this door. I have no idea where it might lead in the future, but I have learned this: God is in control and all I need to do is be faithful and obedient, keep myself humble, remain clean and ready, and, most of all, wait upon God, whose timing is always perfect.

Nine

THE ANTICIPATION
OF ETERNITY

*For our light affliction, which is but for a moment,
is working for us a far more exceeding and eternal weight
of glory, while we do not look at the things which are seen,
but at the things which are not seen. For the things
which are seen are temporary, but the things
which are not seen are eternal.*

— 2 CORINTHIANS 4:17–18 NKJV

No, I don't know the future, but I do know this:
the best is yet to be! Heaven awaits us,
and that will be far, far more glorious than
anything we can ever imagine.

— BILLY GRAHAM

THE ANTICIPATION
OF ETERNITY

Forever. It's a word that demands that we pause and ponder. We can't fully comprehend the meaning of the word *forever,* because we are limited by time. This is one reason that it is so difficult for so many nonbelievers to cope with death. The idea that a person continues to exist beyond this life—beyond the grave—is inconceivable to many of them. They take greater comfort in believing that when someone dies, the person ceases to exist, than they do in the idea of death without finality. It may be comforting for some to believe that way, but it's untrue.

The Bible clearly states that God has determined that every human being who has ever lived or ever will live is destined to exist forever in one of two places: in heaven with Him, or in hell with the devil and his demons. For the true believer, there is the promise of eternal paradise in the presence of God. Those who reject Christ's message of salvation will face an eternity of punishment for their sin.

I want to focus in this chapter on eternity and what true believers have to look forward to. I want to discuss what the Bible tells about heaven and what awaits those of us who have been truly converted. Most of all, I want to give the reader a glimpse of the joy and anticipation I now have as I look forward to "forever" in the presence of God.

IT'S A WONDERFUL ETERNITY

The most important truth about heaven is that God will be there. God the Father, God the Son, and God the Holy Spirit will be there, enjoying perfect fellowship with one another and with us. Our perfect fellowship with God—which was broken back in the Garden of Eden—will be restored, and we will look forward to an eternity of perfect harmony with our Creator. We will live forever as the eternal children of God the Father, who chose us to be His before the foundation of the world. The Bible tells us that we will become brothers and sisters to the Lord Jesus Christ (Mark 3:35). As the church, we will be His perfect bride (Revelation 19:7; 21:9).

Because heaven will be perfect, we will enjoy unmarred communion with the triune God. Free at last from sin and evil, we will be holy as our God is holy. The Bible tells us that sin will have been destroyed forever, so that it can never again enter God's creation.

I believe heaven will be like falling in love with God in such a way that all other relationships pale in comparison. When we see Jesus Christ face-to-face, our joy will be beyond understanding, and we will be overcome with awe and consumed in worship.

I believe when we get to heaven, we will receive an understanding of God's plan and purpose for all that happened to us while we lived on earth. I believe it could be similar to what took place in one of my favorite movies, *It's a Wonderful Life*. This movie portrays the life of George Bailey, who is suffering through a crisis that causes him to question his reason for living. The movie opens with a scene of heaven, where people are praying for God to come

to George Bailey's rescue. As the story progresses, an angel is sent to help George, who has declared that it would
have been better had he never been born. At this point,
Clarence, the angel sent to help George, shows him how
the world would have been different without him. Clarence
allows him to see the impact he has had on his family and
friends and the entire town.

My favorite point in the movie is when Clarence takes
George to the graveyard at his hometown of Pottersfield.
There, George sees the tombstone of his younger brother,
Harry Bailey, who drowned when he was eight years old because George had never been born and thus was not there
to rescue him from an icy pond. Harry never went to war
and never became an ace pilot who shot down an enemy
plane that subsequently sank a navy transport ship with
thousands of soldiers on board.

As George reflects on these discoveries, Clarence asks
him, "George Bailey, don't you see you had a wonderful
life?" Toward the end of the movie, George cries out to
God to give him back his life, even with its problems.

Of course, this movie is fiction. It is not necessarily
based on sound biblical doctrine. Still, I believe there are
some profound truths in the story, truths that can encourage us to put our earthly existence in an eternal perspective.

When we get to heaven, we will see our various hard-
ships and failures and the pain we endured from God's perspective. We will see how He used all those things to carry
out His purpose and plan for our lives. We will each see
how God used our lives as jewels to be displayed on His
great mosaic, which will be viewed for all of eternity as a
demonstration of the beauty of a life in Christ. I believe we
will see the impact of our lives on others, and we will see

how God used us to build His kingdom. Every good deed we ever did will be displayed, and every act of kindness and its effect will be revealed.

I believe the height of our story, though, will be when we come to understand all that God did to bring about our salvation. We will see the people who prayed for us and those who preached and witnessed to us. We will see how God providentially ordered our steps so that the Holy Spirit could implant within us a heart of faith, then quicken that heart to a new life in Christ.

What a joy it will be to witness and learn about the salvation of each of God's saints. I believe that upon hearing and seeing each of these stories, the population of heaven will shout and sing praises and worship to God. I believe this will go on and on for millions of years, each chronicle providing a piece of the picture that God is using to unfold His eternal plan and the wisdom and perfection of all of His ways.

It is hard to fathom the joy and ecstasy this experience will bring. I believe it will surpass even the joy we feel in this life when we hear of how God brought a believer to saving faith.

A FOCUS ON ETERNITY

It is tragic that many believers are so caught up with this world and with their "idols" that they scarcely think about heaven. They are content to dwell in the rubble of this sin-ridden world, rather than dwell on eternity, where we will forever learn of our God and all the great things He has done.

The world we live in today is consumed with its chase

after paradise. People think they can find it in money and power, in sex and beauty, or in the pursuit of other pleasures. They strive to find their own paradise, only to discover that it wasn't what they thought it would be.

The truth of the matter is that we lost paradise—perfect fellowship with God—at the Fall, and we will not see it again until we arrive at that great city of God, the New Jerusalem. That new paradise is heaven, and it will last forever.

We who are truly in Christ can but imagine what awaits us in heaven. The apostle Paul tells us that God's paradise is too wonderful for words:

> *Eye has not seen, nor ear heard,*
> *Nor have entered into the heart of man*
> *The things which God has prepared*
> *for those who love Him.*
> (1 CORINTHIANS 2:9 NKJV)

Ten

THE NEED FOR
REFORMATION AND REVIVAL

"I know all the things you do, and that you have a
reputation for being alive—but you are dead. Now wake
up! Strengthen what little remains, for even what is left is at
the point of death. . . . I know all the things you do, that you
are neither hot nor cold. I wish you were one or the other!
But since you are like lukewarm water,
I will spit you out of my mouth!"

— REVELATION 3:1–2, 15–16

I believe that today in the west, and particularly in America, the new barbarians are all around us. We have bred them in our families and trained them in our classrooms. They inhabit our legislature, our courts, our film studios, and our church. Most of them are attractive and pleasant; their ideas are persuasive and subtle. . . . Today's barbarians are ladies and gentlemen.

— CHUCK COLSON

THE NEED FOR
REFORMATION AND REVIVAL

$\mathcal{A}$s we enter the twenty-first century, I believe that the Christian church is in a greatly needy condition. The body of Christ has serious problems that need to be exposed and confronted. We are in great need of a return to the instruction God provides us in Scripture and of a movement of the Holy Spirit—reformation and revival.

We live in a nation of great prosperity, but a nation that is growing in gross immorality, rampant materialism, and, most of all, blatant disrespect toward God and His Word. What's worse is that many of our churches today are in the same condition as the world around them.

Earlier in this book, I said I believed that the church is currently facing some of the same root problems that brought about the long period of spiritual darkness that led up to the Reformation. Over the course of hundreds of years prior to the Reformation, the church had adopted pagan or nonscriptural practices and ceremonies, added nonbiblical materials to the truth of the Bible, and become preoccupied with religious "externals" rather than what the apostles in the New Testament had laid out for the church. By far, however, the most serious error that developed over that period was the loss of focus on the doctrine of grace. This brought about the addition in the church of requirement of works as assurance of salvation. The church had also set itself up as the intermediary between God and man.

It was in Germany in the early 1500s that God chose to ignite the flame of the Great Reformation, using the stand taken by an obscure monk by the name of Martin Luther. From this simple beginning, God initiated a monumental rescue of His church from its outward shows of formal religious ceremony, as well as rampant corruption among its leadership.

As was the case with the children of Israel when God's glory left the nation (1 Samuel 4), God had withdrawn His presence from the pre-Reformation church, but very few seemed to notice. This condition did not develop overnight, but ever-so-gradually over centuries. Finally, the church had reached the deplorable condition Martin Luther recognized.

History can be a great teacher if we will take time to understand what happened to those who went before us. One of the reasons God gave us the Old Testament was so we could learn what happened to His chosen people, the children of Israel, when they fell away from Him and His Word. As we study the period of the Dark Ages of Europe, we can see how the faith of the early church fathers was lost or corrupted by the world or by neglect of God's Word.

The most significant aspect of the Reformation was a God-initiated movement that led the church to rediscover the fundamental truths of the Bible. These truths came to be known as "Scripture alone" *(sola Scriptura)*, "grace alone" *(sola gratia)*, "Christ alone" *(solus Christus)*, "faith alone" *(sola fide)*, and "God's glory alone" *(soli Deo gloria)*. These truths were the central cries of the reformers and the truths that initiated this great movement of reformation.

HISTORY RELIVED

As was the case in the days leading to the Reformation, one of the great problems of today's church is that we have drifted away from the sound doctrines of the Christian faith. This failure to hold to sound biblical teaching has opened us up to serious error, which in turn has led to a loss of true fellowship, guidance, and power from the triune God.

When the church moves away from the foundational doctrines in Scripture, it gradually but consistently begins to embrace the ways of the world. When this happens, those I refer to as "unconverted believers" gain influence and positions of leadership within the church. This has a weakening and dulling effect on the faith of the truly converted believers who may be vulnerable to becoming lukewarm in their faith.

As this downward spiral continues, the church loses access to the power of God and ceases to be "salt and light" to a lost world. When this happens, lost sinners are not drawn to the wonderful message of the gospel, because its real impact is not clearly visible in those who claim to have it.

TIME FOR REFORMATION!

Too often, the church is consumed not with the true and living God but with self-aggrandizement, self-perpetuation, and self-entertainment. When the church's primary focus is anything but the correct worship of and service to the triune God, it is in a grave position. I believe that is in many ways the position of the church today.

Obviously, something needs to change.

If the church is to get back to its primary focus and mission, there must be an outbreak of true spiritual revival across all of Christendom. This would involve a stirring of the Holy Spirit, which would bring millions under the conviction of sin and cause them to cry out to God for help and mercy. Those who have left their first love and grown lukewarm in their faith would come under a great conviction to repent and rededicate their lives to their Lord and Savior. Even devoted followers of Christ would be brought to their knees as they were convicted of areas in their lives where they have drifted or not been all they should have been.

It is only by this process that the church will be rescued and reformed. This will begin with one person at a time. Martin Luther did not know that God was using him to start the Reformation of the Christian church; he just knew he needed to be in right standing before God. At one point, Luther wasn't sure he was truly on his way to heaven because he didn't know if he had done enough to earn his way. Finally, God opened his eyes to the truth that had been lost on Luther and on the church: that justification is by faith alone, and that salvation is *all* of God. It was Luther's knowledge of the Word of God combined with the illumination by the Holy Spirit that triggered the change in him, and that ultimately led to the formation of the Protestant church.

Today, we need godly and humble people to continually warn the church of the dangers and tragedies that lie ahead if we don't alter our present course and bring ourselves in line with God's Word.

My mind frequently returns to one of the first Bible study courses that I took. It was on the Old Testament book of Amos. I am still amazed at how relevant the message from God, through this simple goat herder, is for our present day. One of the references in this book is to God's plumb line (Amos 7:7–8). A plumb line is what engineers and construction people use to make certain that everything stays exactly straight vertically. Amos was sent to show those of the Northern Kingdom how far off they had strayed from the commandments of the Lord, how far they were from "plumb" with His commandments.

Today, God's plumb line for His people is the Bible. His written Word is His acceptable standard, His measurement of truth. Sadly, much of what is promoted as "Christian" today will not meet this standard. Even the truly converted have fallen prey to believing that the Scriptures are somehow not totally sufficient, that we need other ideas and approaches to deal with life. How far we have strayed from Psalm 19, which tells us of the value of God's Word and the truth that it contains.

If reformation and revival are to come, we must make certain that all we do, in word and in deed, stands up to the standard of God's Word. It is only the appropriation and application of the Scriptures that can bring about true reformation and revival. For this reason, it is important that each of us as true believers knows what the Word of God says. Every believer needs to make certain he or she is actively reading, studying, and applying the Word of God. When that happens, God can use each of us to fuel the flame of reformation and revival.

Conclusion

THE NEED TO
EXAMINE OURSELVES

*Examine yourselves to see whether you are in the faith;
test yourselves. Do you not realize that Christ Jesus is
in you—unless, of course, you fail the test?*

2 CORINTHIANS 13:5 NIV

I must understand what it means to be a counterfeit Christian. The Bible reveals many—Judas, Demas, Diotrephes—and so does human experience. I have known a number of "saints" who no longer walk with God. This is enough to chill me with fear, then drive me to my knees in self-examination.

— W. GLYN EVANS

THE NEED TO
EXAMINE OURSELVES

$\mathcal{A}$ lot of things in my life changed after I came to saving faith in the Lord Jesus Christ.

Just a few months after my new birth, I began to feel a strong leading from the Holy Spirit to leave my career in the medical health industry. At first the leadings were very gentle, but after a time it became clear that God was guiding me in a different direction.

About the time I had decided to leave my position with the company in Germany, I was scheduled to meet with my boss in Hanover. I knew it would present the perfect opportunity for me to deliver my resignation in person, which I did. My boss was stunned that I would leave a career that I was not only successful in, but that I truly loved. We talked more as we boarded a flight for Munich, and as we continued our talk on the airplane, I had a chance to tell my boss about what God had done in my life.

Shortly before we landed, my boss looked at me and remarked, "Well, all I can say is that I really don't understand what has happened to you. But I know that you have found something that most people spend their whole life looking for but never find. To be honest, I envy you."

I truly had found something most people never find, and that is the new life that comes from an encounter with the living God of the Bible. I had been dead in my sins, but

I had experienced a true encounter with the living God of the Bible. God brought me to life spiritually by the power of the Holy Spirit. In my case God chose to use many different circumstances to open my eyes to sin and to show me that nothing can set us free from sin but the truth. That truth begins in the Bible with what God has revealed to us about Himself, about our fallen condition, and about what He has done to provide a solution for that condition through Jesus Christ's death on the cross.

I was reborn from above, converted, and regenerated, and I was on my way not just to an eternity in heaven with the Lord, but to a life of true joy and fulfillment.

When I came to a true saving faith in Jesus, I immediately realized that the god I had been serving all those years as a professing Christian was not the true and living God, but a god of my own making. From that morning of October 12, 1980, on, I have been learning more and more about this wonderful God of the Bible. And the more I have learned about Him, the more in awe of Him I have become. And the more in awe of Him I become, the more I understand just how lost I was before I was truly born again. As I have grown in my faith, I have become more and more aware of sinfulness—my own and that of those around me—and of the devastation of sin.

I have also come to a realization of the potential for evil and self-deception in the unconverted heart. As God shed His light into my heart, I became aware of the presence of my own sinful behavior before a holy and righteous God. I was overwhelmed with grief and sadness when I realized how deceived I had been all those years when I thought I was a true believer but was still lost in my sin. Tragically, a vast number of people who attend church regularly still live in their sinful condition and, like I was, are blinded to that fact.

It is not easy for someone in his mid-thirties to be born again and truly converted. That's because the longer someone is away from the Lord's presence, the harder his or her heart can become to the things of God. I'm grateful to tell you that all things are possible with God. He reached down to me and saved me, a man at that time in his life.

The Bible warns us that there are three great forces that pull us toward sin: the world, the flesh, and the devil. It is only the true child of God who can have victory over these strong sinful forces. I can tell you that from the time I was truly converted, God's presence has been there to help me at every point of struggle with sin.

My growth in Christ has been an adventure, one that only a true child of God can understand and appreciate. I have suffered through many setbacks and failures. So many times I have missed the mark, yet my God is faithful. I push forward, knowing that I can trust Him to keep His promise to complete the work He began in me.

I have found the "pearl of great price." I have found that which everyone longs for. I have found the true love, joy, and peace that comes only from a true relationship with Jesus Christ. And I long to see others come to know what it is to be a true believer.

My testimony of what the Lord has done in my life is just one of countless examples of what happens when a sinner is saved and given new life in Christ. I can say with assurance that I am a child of God. That is because I believe God's promises, and it's because of the evidence of His presence in my life.

How about you? Have you truly been born again? Has

God, through His Holy Spirit, truly converted you and begun that process of renewal and regeneration?

Before you answer these questions, take some time to examine your life and ask yourself if it truly reflects the presence of the living God. Take the time to think about the following questions:

1. Do you really know and serve God as He has revealed Himself in the Bible, or have you trivialized God by playing religious games with a god of your own creation?

2. Have you come to see that the root cause of everything bad is what the Bible calls evil, which is a manifestation of pride? Are you confronting the evil that resides in your own heart?

3. Do you see the plague of sin that is rampant in our world, and do you see that everyone—including yourself—is guilty before a holy and righteous God, or are you still comfortable with your sins?

4. Have you been truly born again from above by a supernatural act of God, or are you simply using the label of *Christian?*

5. Have you experienced true conversion which comes from repentance toward God and faith in Jesus Christ, or do you remain an unconverted believer?

6. Have the eyes of your mind been opened to the truth of God that has been given to us by the Holy Spirit in the Bible, or are you still blinded to this truth?

7. Have you become a new creation in Christ, where old things are gone and new things are present, or are you living in many ways just like the world around you?

8. Are you being changed as you learn to wait on God

as He works His plans for your life, or are you really your own boss?

9. Are your thoughts more and more toward spending eternity with God, or are you still consumed with the world?

10. Are you still on the broad road that leads to destruction, or have you found the narrow way?

If you can answer these questions positively and with great conviction and assurance, it is because the Holy Spirit testifies that you are truly a converted believer, a true child of Almighty God, and on your way to heaven. On the other hand, if you have doubts about where you truly stand with the triune God of the Bible, then I would invite you to get on your knees and cry out to God for help and for answers. It is God alone who holds the key to eternal life and to heaven.

I want to finish by giving you these encouraging words:

"Seek, and you will find; knock, and it will be opened"
(MATTHEW 7:7 NKJV).

"Call to Me, and I will answer you"
(JEREMIAH 33:3 NKJV).

*"Come to Me, all you who labor and are heavy laden,
and I will give you rest"*
(MATTHEW 11:28 NKJV).

Moody Press and William Thrasher welcome you on-line!

If you have appreciated William Thrasher's message and are interested in investigating the topic further, we direct you on-line. Moody Press takes you on a journey which will explore insights from the Bible and Mr. Thrasher's experiences.

www.moodypress.org/promo/thingsivelearned/

More Directions for Your Spiritual Journey.

William L. Thrasher, Jr. continues the tradition he began with his acclaimed *Basics for Believers*, challenging those new to the Christian life and those who have walked the path for years to learn and apply the basic tenets of the faith. He addresses the topics of what we see, hear, read, think and say (and many more), and helps us learn how these affect who we are.

ISBN: 0-8024-3744-3, Paperback

"Bill Thrasher keeps on gracing us with books that go to the heart of the Christian life. This will be a life-changing read for many."
— Kent Hughes, Pastor, College Church in Wheaton, IL

"Here is an opportunity for us to be introduced to the great themes of Christianity in bite-sized pieces. You will want to share this book with many."
— Erwin W. Lutzer, Senior Pastor, The Moody Church

"Basics for Believers, Volume 2 *answers a crying need for the church to-day. It is both interesting and accurate; the style is as simple as these truths are profound."*
— From the foreword by John MacArthur

Suggested Reading
by William L. Thrasher, Jr.

God has left us a single, trustworthy source that reveals who He is. His purpose. His love. His desire to transform history, nations—and especially the lives of everyday people who will take Him at His word, the Bible. Erwin Lutzer's revealing book can help you discover the Bible for the first time and give you—and every person who wants to trust God—compelling reasons to explore.

ISBN #0-8024-8442-5, Paperback,Christian Living

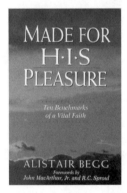

The prayer that pleases God is larger than ourselves. It focuses on the glory of God and remembers the needs of others. The life that is truly fulfilling gives back to God the talents and abilities He has given us to be used for His glory. Alistair Begg applies these principles to ten areas of our lives and challenges us to experience our Father's pleasure as we glorify Him.

ISBN #0-8024-7138-2, Hardcover, Christian Living

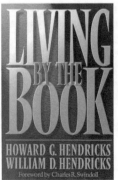

What's the secret to gleaning wisdom and enthusiasm from reading Scripture passages? Howard Hendricks knows that the "secret" really is no secret at all. It is simply a case of practicing effective Bible study methods. But to practice them you must know them. And that's where Howard Hendricks and his son Bill can enlighten you and show you the steps to living by the Book.

ISBN: 0-8024-0816-8, Paperback, Biblical Reference/Bible Study